TASTY REVIEWS

You Are Who You Eat ... The Revolutionary New Cannibal Diet

"OMG! To all my Facebook peeps — you've got to try this diet! It's the original Paleo!"
Marcy Hanson, Planet's Best Diets Blogger

"This is so true!...Wait a minute. Is this tongue in cheek? Whose tongue? Whose cheek?"
Oswella Parsons, Housewife, Patterson, NJ

"Mighty tasty!"
Larry Yurdin, President, Yurdin Entertainment

"My guests and I laughed ourselves silly. Well, I did. My guests stopped when they saw the way my hot tub's tricked out."
Harry Hanson, Event Planner, Albuquerque, NM

"I've already lost 10 pounds. *This* is the way to profile perps!"
Francis Ragout, Police Detective, New York, NY

"Cannibal jokes? Ewwww! ....Have you heard the one about why Cannibals don't like clowns? They taste funny."
#SomeOfMyBestFriendsAreCannibals

ALSO BY THE AUTHORS

1960   Vegetables *Can* Be Fun!

1970   Advanced Sprout Cookery

1980   101 Ways with Chicken Wings

1990   Frogs Legs Do *Not* Taste Just Like Chicken!

1996   Liver Fantasies

1999   Herbs of Man, with Dedini

2003   Wines for the Cannibal Connoisseur

2006   Crockpot Cookery for the Cannibal Kitchen, with Dedini

2008   Crockpot Cookery, the Sequel to *Crockpot*

2010   Adapting to the Microwave

2012   Alternate Meals for the Cannibal Frequent Flyer

                Published simultaneously with the sensational article, *A Practical Guide for the Airlines to Saving Fuel Costs through Lightening Weight Loads en Route*

2014   Where the Meals Are – A Hunters' Guide to Travel and Entertainment

YOU ARE WHO YOU EAT

The Revolutionary New Cannibal Diet

By Ina Silvert Hillebrandt, with Uncle Dan

Cover Art and Illustrations by Dedini

You Are Who You Eat
The Revolutionary New Cannibal Diet

By Ina Silvert Hillebrandt, with Uncle Dan Silvert

Cover art and illustrations by Dedini
Cover and Interior Design by Ina Hillebrandt

Published by Pawpress

For information on reprints, bulk purchase, or available related performance and merchandising properties, and licensing questions, please contact the publisher:
Pawpress
Brentwood Village ● P.O. Box 492213
Los Angeles, CA 90049
http://InasPawprints.com. Changing in 2016 to http://Inahill.com

Library of Congress Control Number: 2015918016

a PAWPRESS book
Printed in the U.S.A.

THE CANNIBAL MOTTO:
To eat his own

Dedication

To my father, Abe Silvert, who started the tradition of Cannibal jokes many years ago. We always knew one was coming when, as he was driving, he would stop mid-sentence, suddenly silent. After a minute or two, out would come a new Cannibal joke, just as we knew it would. This new edition is also dedicated to the wonderful Eldon Dedini and Uncle Dan, both of whom tossed many bone mots into the pot, but unfortunately left for a higher plate before the revised version was fully cooked.

Foreword

Have you been *seriously* trying to lose weight? Forever? O.K. Are you ready to throw out your preconceptions and try something totally different? Then you may be ready to join the millions who swear by this extraordinary new diet, adapted for the modern kitchen, from Papua, New Guinea!

After all, have you ever seen a fat Cannibal in the old country?

Marietta Mandible
Renowned Cannibal Weight Control Expert
and Restaurant Critic

Acknowledgements

A huge thanks, first, to Ms. Marietta Mandible. Without her pioneering approach to weight loss — including tips on how to enjoy food while maintaining a svelte bod — and her extraordinary generosity in sharing her knowledge with us, this book could never have been written.

Thanks also to Ina's daughter, Nicole Hillebrandt, for her laughter and groans, clear clues as to what to leave in or toss out, and patience in listening to many stories. And to our aunt/sister Sophie Silvert, who inspired the writing down of the jokes. And to Mom and Pop Fran and Gus Syken, for laughing with us.

And thanks to the many friends who encouraged us, generously gave us ideas and the support to stay with it — Jeff Levenson, Gerry Fried, Mark Evens, John Bragin, Don Safran, Ruth Chadsey, Nadya Guisi, Harvey Bondar, Joe Kaplan, Ruth and Mike Edmonds, Jill Hannum, Ramon Jose, Jane Phillips, Larry Walsh, Larry Yurdin, Helcio Milito, Bob Lucky, Rob Patterson, Marvin Wolf, Joanna Fancy and Anita Alberts. Special thanks to Gail Allison. Also to Sara Bernstein, and to Jim Wanless, for energy on the wild side. And Todd Liebman, for his bonhomie and cooking utensil guidance.

YOU ARE WHO YOU EAT

The Revolutionary New Cannibal Diet

By Ina Silvert Hillebrandt, with Uncle Dan

Cover Art and Illustrations by Dedini

ROOMMATES COME
ROOMMATES GO

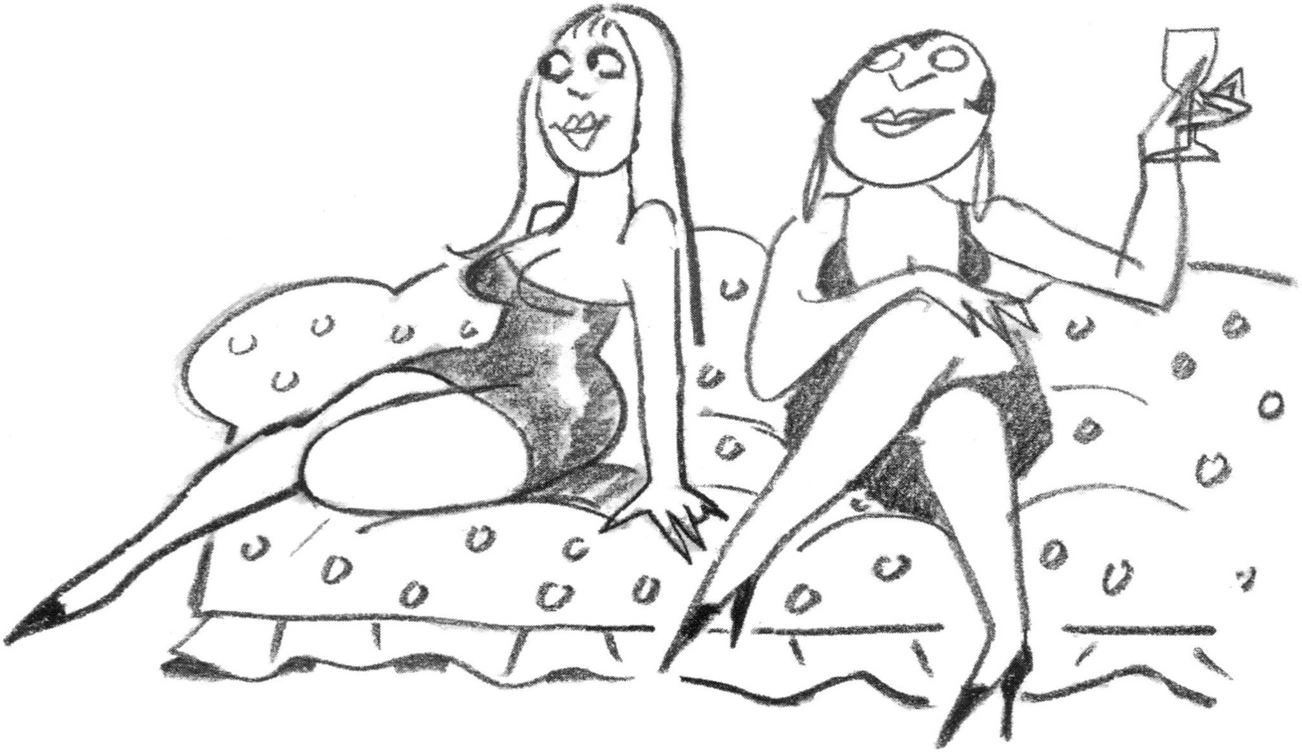

CONTENTS

"FIRST WE GET RID OF THE LAWYERS. THEY'RE INDIGESTIBLE."

INTRODUCTION

Welcome! Whether you've come to us from the Cannibal or Civilian population, if you have a problem getting and keeping your weight down, have we got a diet for you!

First, as Ms. Mandible notes in her preface, we've modernized the original New Guinean eating plan. In the wild, we Cannibals were never fat! But after emigrating to the "civilized" world, a number of us absorbed some of its cultural downsides. Consequently, now there are as many of us needing to watch who we eat as there are among the civilians constantly battling girth.

But, we're happy to report, just as the modern world taketh, it also giveth — in spades. Thus, we've been able to pepper our books with revolutionary discoveries in nutrition and food preparation. You'll learn why eating Wright, and other families from the new organic breeding farms, will make you not only healthier, but svelte. You'll find cooking and preparation tips, such as using Oil of Olé when sautéing Spaniards, to help you whip up your own healthful and slimming meals and snacks.

Ms. Mandible also teaches us that a successful weight loss plan should really be viewed as a way of life rather than a diet. And to stay on track, it's important to pamper and nurture yourself as you go. So we've included ideas for uplifting your spirits while you munch more healthily. You'll find which plays and movies, such as "The Guest Who Came To Be Dinner" (a hilarious farce about mistaken entrées), are "must sees," music to cook by, psychiatric news, and many other tidbits our adopted culture offers us for beefing up our mental and emotional state, fortifying us to avoid succumbing to eating the wrong people.

Remember our two rules of thumb. First, avoid eating same. Second, if our food plan puts you a bit on the fence morally, think about this: what's more important, scruples or being thin?

VEGETARIAN CANNIBAL SURPRISED AT LUNCH

CANNIBAL HEALTH TIPS

With all of the information today on proper nutrition, the modern Cannibal can be assured not only of losing weight, but of living a much healthier and longer life! Here are some terrific new weight control principles we've gathered from all over the world.

Lay off fried people.

Look for the new low cholesterol treat:

    Toe-fu.

An idea to consider: Some people have developed very narrow, but healthy, tastes. Monica Lewinski, for example, dines only on Heads of State.

Check your next meal for high cholesterol levels: make sure he has eaten a low fat diet.

Eschew accessories: The first epidemic of mononucleosis among Cannibals was traced to a feast where a former famous German film star, Eryk Fun Strawheim, monocle and all, was the entrée. Today's gastronomes are well advised to check for spectacles and such before cooking.

Eat Wright, and other families from the new organic breeding farms. These non-GMO, pesticide- and hormone-free foods are ideal for our health!

A somewhat surprising note:

A smart Cannibal seeks out people with sour dispositions. He knows enough to go easy on sweets.

.

You might want to be on the lookout for the new health food book classic:

To Serve Mankind

Cannibals should refrain from eating brains. You never know what stupid ideas you could absorb.

"REMEMBER - EAT THE PROTEIN BEFORE THE PROTEIN EATS YOU!"

CHART OF FOOD VALUES
Per ½ Pound Portion

	Calories	Fat	Carbos	Protein	Texture	Taste
Nun	400	0	0	50 g	Fibrous	On the dry side: Lots of starch
New York Banker	2,000	10,000 g	0	0	Chewy	Greasy
Southern Californian	500	0	100 g	20 g	Flaky	Lean, Flavorful. Best served with sprouts

CHART OF FOOD VALUES
Per ½ Pound Portion

	Calories	Fat	Carbos.	Protein	Texture	Taste
Southern Senator	1,500	5,000 g	100 g	40 g	Fluffy	Very airy texture. Laced with fat. Hushpuppies make good side dish.
British Aristocrat	1,000	0 g	50 g	60 g	Tough and sinewy	Best with popovers, au jus gravy and Yorkshire pudding.
Corporate Head Hunter	1,700	2,500 g	400 g	30 g	Slick	Hard-boiled best.

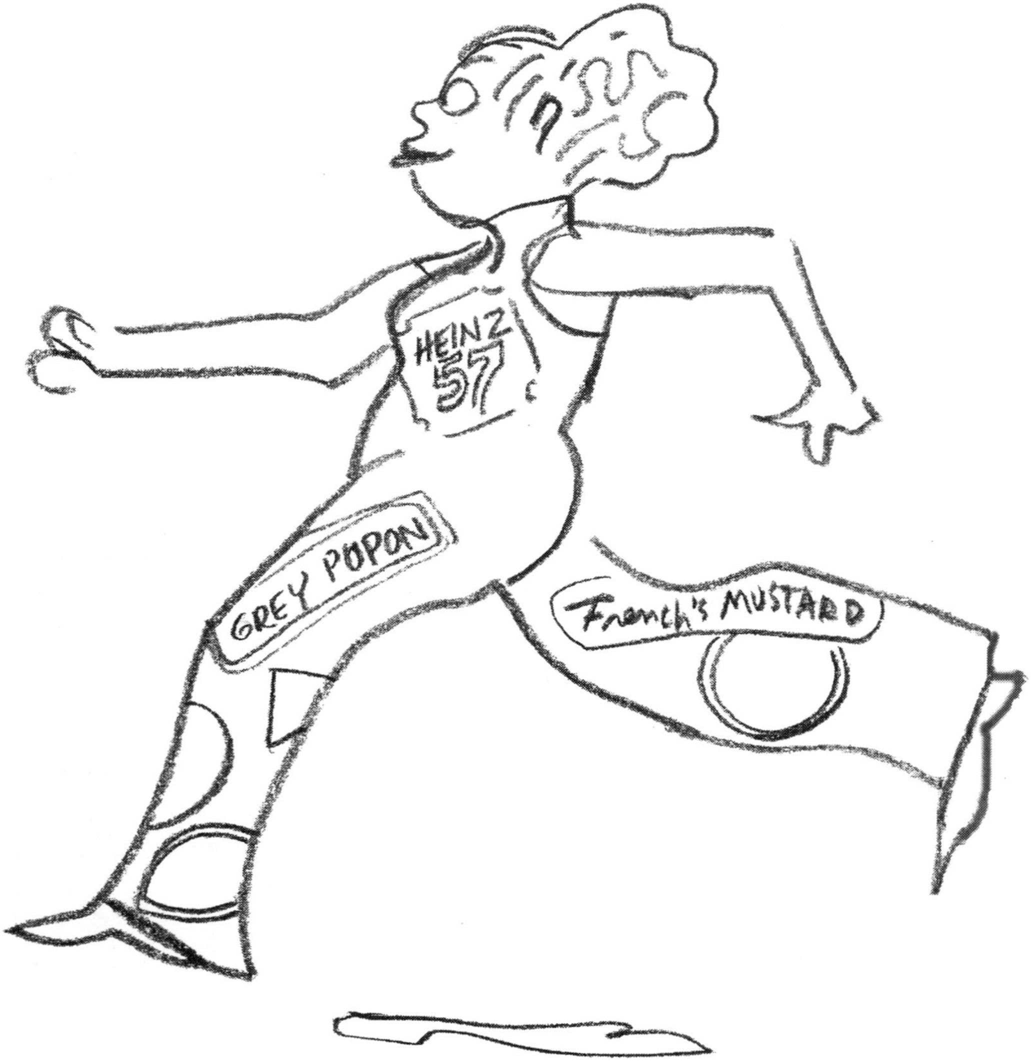
HEINZ
57
GREY POUPON
French's MUSTARD

COOKING TIPS

We urge you to try these healthful and delicious preparation and seasoning techniques for dishes from different backgrounds and faraway lands.

Spaniards: Very tasty. Best broiled. Use Oil of Olé generously. Chef should wear bright red apron. For some reason this enhances the flavor.

Greeks, Italians and Mediterraneans: In general, this group is naturally flavorful. Never add olives or olive oil. Very little, if any, seasoning necessary.

Corsicans: Known as the psychedelic or LSD of foods. Devotees of this food wear three corner hats, love military parades and ribbons, and are sure they own Versailles.

Referees: Distinguishable by their stripes. Another gamy dish. Prepare as with gamblers.

Politicians and Lawyers: First remove calloused, tough hides. Steaming, parboiling renders meat tender. Add sprigs of parsley, whole onions dotted with cloves to pot to transform these types into tasty dishes.

Televangelists: Inedible. Discard.

Gamblers: Can be appetizing, especially if marinated overnight and baked in slow oven. Also, be sure to use enough seasoning to remove their gaminess.

Scandinavians: Widely recommended by the Health Food Industry. Low in cholesterol and fat. Only drawbacks are characteristic salty, fishy flavor. Soak overnight in refrigerator, then boil with bay leaf and oregano. Serve warm or chilled with lemon wedges and tartar or cocktail sauce.

BALLERINA LEGS TASTE JUST LIKE FROG LEGS

MORE COOKING TIPS...

Masters of ceremonies: Fine for luncheon. Best served on toast with melted cheddar.

After-Dinner Speakers: Usually very bland. Season well.

MUAMMAR GADDAFI's
TUMS

Comedians: Often tasteless. Treat as above.

TV Reporters: Set oven on warm and roast several hours. They are generally half-baked.

Used Car Salesmen: Tongues widely regarded as most desirable parts. Remainder inferior. Best not used.

Realtors: Leave a lot to be desired. Go lightly on the salt cellar.

Eskimo: Serve chilled. Great with salads.

Jockeys: Perfect breakfast food. Goes well with oatmeal. Make sure you stirrup well.

Salesmen: Take a long time in cooking. Set your pressure cooker on high.

Policemen: An acquired taste. Not your average chicken's dinner. Pound with mallet 'til tender before baking.

Rear Admirals: Great for rump steaks.

Ballet Dancers: Some fans of this exotic food swear by it. Others find it tough and sinewy. A toss-up.

And remember... You *can* have safe sex parts as long as you remember to use condiments!

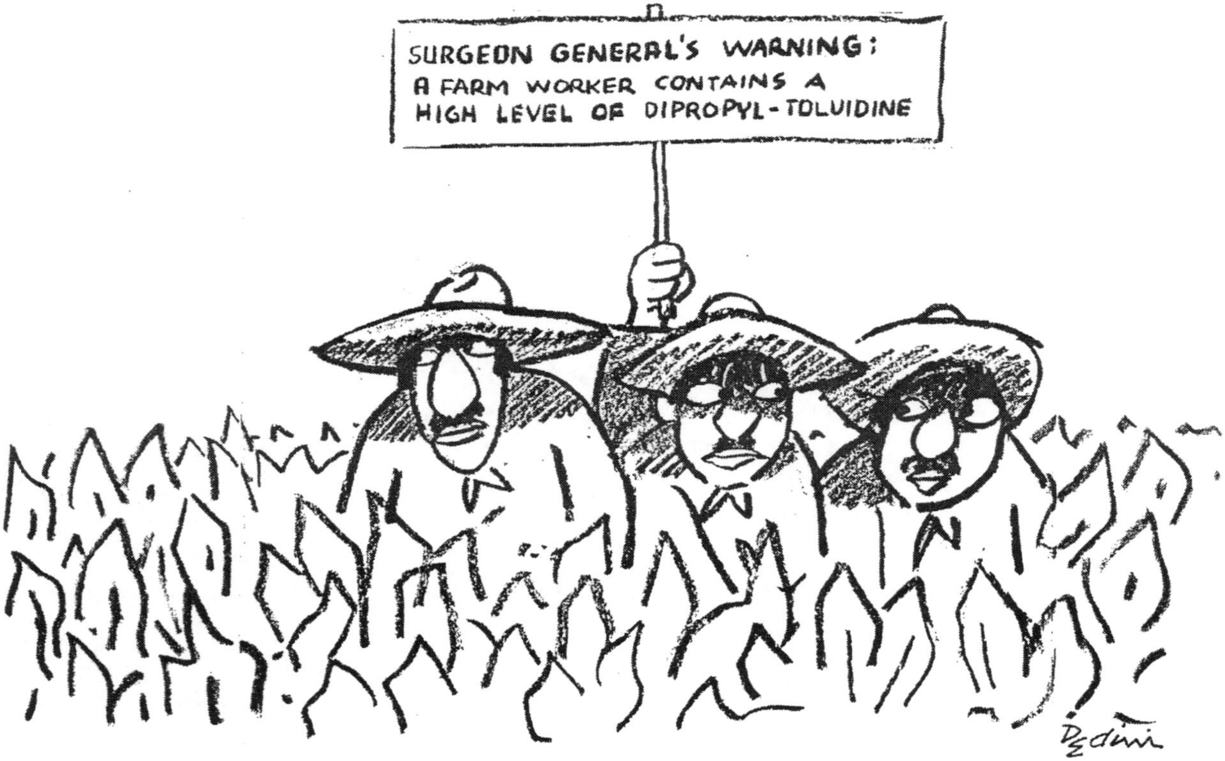
SURGEON GENERAL'S WARNING:
A FARM WORKER CONTAINS A
HIGH LEVEL OF DIPROPYL-TOLUIDINE
DEDINI

IN THE NEWS

CP* June 12: Fresno, CA. Kokuit Chavez is very worried about a terrible habit the tribes have been exhibiting — eating people who have been exposed to high levels of pesticides. As a result, he is mounting an important crusade to boycott catching and eating farm workers.

Advertising Roundup

Look for the new art magazine, soon to be published: ***The Erotic Cannibal.***

Kids!

UCI**, August 18: Washington, D.C. The Cannibal tribal elders and medicine men of the Tartuff tribe report extreme agitation over recent trends among their youth. Increasingly, they are perturbed as the youngsters mock tradition. The teens often gather together, eating vegetables; at times, even carrots. On certain occasions, strange odors permeate the air — cabbage or cauliflower cooking. Crude cooking instruments are used in these ritual eviscerations of custom. Battered steamers have been found later by the elders at the cook sites, along with tattered copies of *Prevention Magazine*. Well-thumbed Burpee seed catalogs are in evidence. Finally, this appeal from the tribal leadership, sent by smoke signal, messengers and tom-toms:

JUST SAY NO TO VEGGIES!

*Cannibal Press
**United Cannibal International

14

Harvard Review of Medicine, Dateline Atlanta CCDC* December 24: New disease among Cannibals recently discovered — human brains carry a deadly virus. Oddly enough, it causes the eater to die laughing. The disease has to incubate for thirty years. So smart Cannibals at age 60 are eating brains, so they can go out laughing.

Washington Post CE**, October 31: White House Chef I. Marinate whipped up a fiery new creation today — Eye of Newt, aged in genuine pork barrels. Most felt it was the perfect food for Halloween. However, informed sources report that the dish earned mixed reviews on reflection. Some diners loved it — the bold flavors left them energized, feisty and with a renewed sense that haute cuisine is (and should be) the opiate of the rich. Others were on the opposite side of The House; the dish reminded them of recycled pablum, with a nasty aftertaste to boot. The chef, wishing to please his regulars, said he will be revisiting the recipe in the coming year.

New York Times, September 18: The GOTBP (Grand Old Tea Baggers Party) insisted today that they have absolutely no intention of draining all Congress members' bathtubs. "It's the *government* we want to see trickle down," they assured former Speaker Boner and other members of The House and Senate. Informed sources report that many members of Congress appeared to be confused rather than comforted by the GOTBP's policy statement, and remain concerned for the future of their own -- and their families' -- hygiene. All declined to comment for this article.

---

*Cannibal Centers for Disease Control
**Cannibal Edition

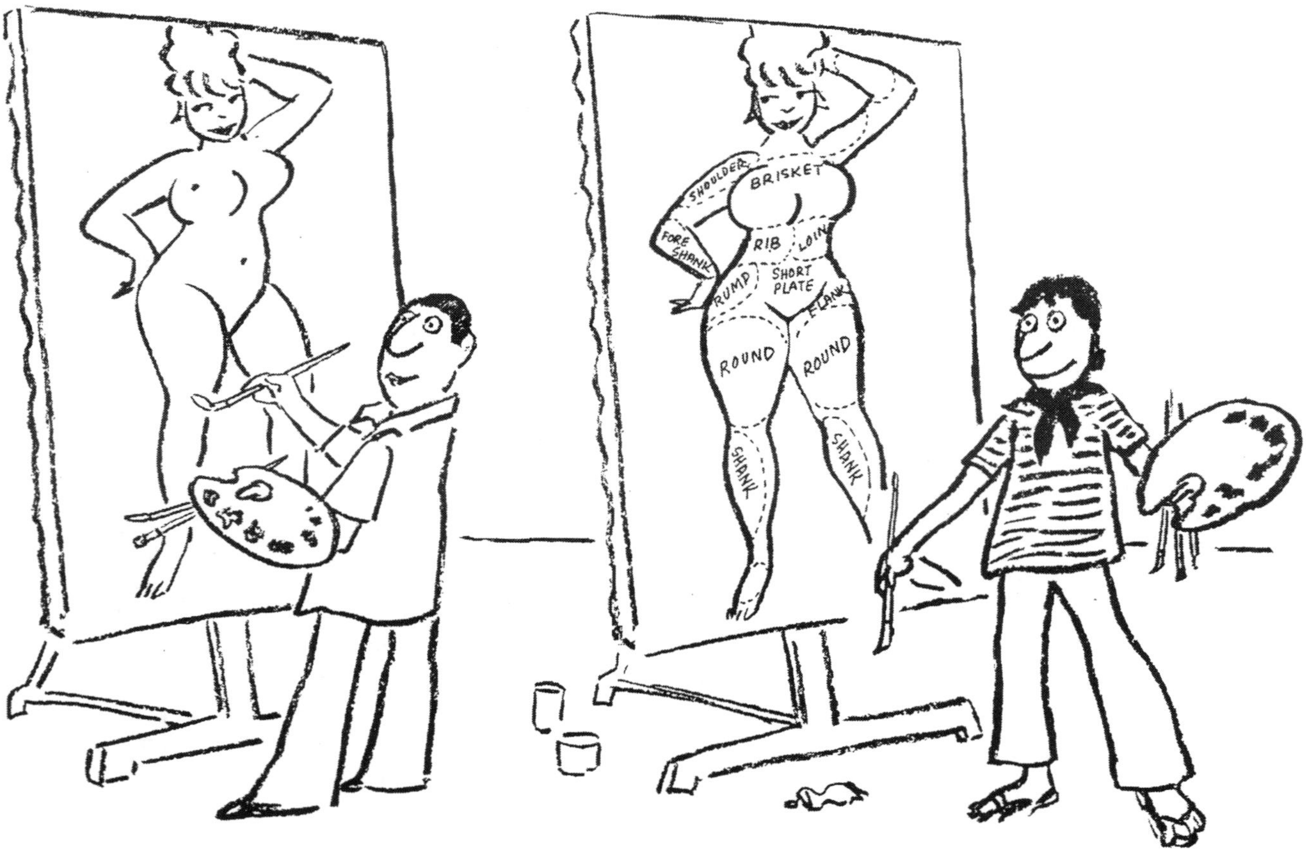
SHOULDER
BRISKET
FORE SHANK
RIB
LOIN
RUMP
SHORT PLATE
FLANK
ROUND
ROUND
SHANK
SHANK

THE LIVELY CANNIBAL ARTS

Losing weight does not have to be all hard work and deprivation! In fact, as Ms. Mandible has taught as, and as we touched upon in our introduction, it's important to pamper and nurture yourself while dieting. So we've included some ideas for uplifting your spirits as you score — and dine upon — more healthy foodstuffs.

Check out our reviews for exciting Museum Visits, must-see Movies and Plays — such as *The Accidental Hors d' Oeuvre,* and Music To Cook By. Book Reviews and a Dining Out Guide round out our suggestions for cultural enjoyment, and Famous Sayings and Cannibal Classics add bone mots to toss out at parties.

Museums

A visit to the National Cannsonian Museum in Washington, D.C., reveals many exciting and inspirational exhibits. Some of the treasures on permanent display include the following:

- A scrap of foolscap, recently unearthed in Upper Bagshot, England, found in situ at a prehistoric Cannibal feast site, which greatly excited archaeologists at the dig. Only a few words remain:

  Alas, poor Yorick. I stewed him well.

- Relics of Cannibal saints.

- A remarkable collection of bone toothpicks.

IVAN THE TERRIBLE'S NAPKIN

- A breath-taking, somewhat different, picture of The Last Supper.

● Works of the legendary playwright, Shakespygmy, that have withstood the test of time.

THE MERCHANT OF VENISON

MACBETH BURGERS

HAMLETTE

ANTHONY BASTES CLEOPATRA

HENRY ATE

- And finally, on our museum must-see recommendations, the scattered sonnets.

"HOW SHALL I COOK THEE? LET ME COUNT THE WAYS."
ELIZABETH BROWNED

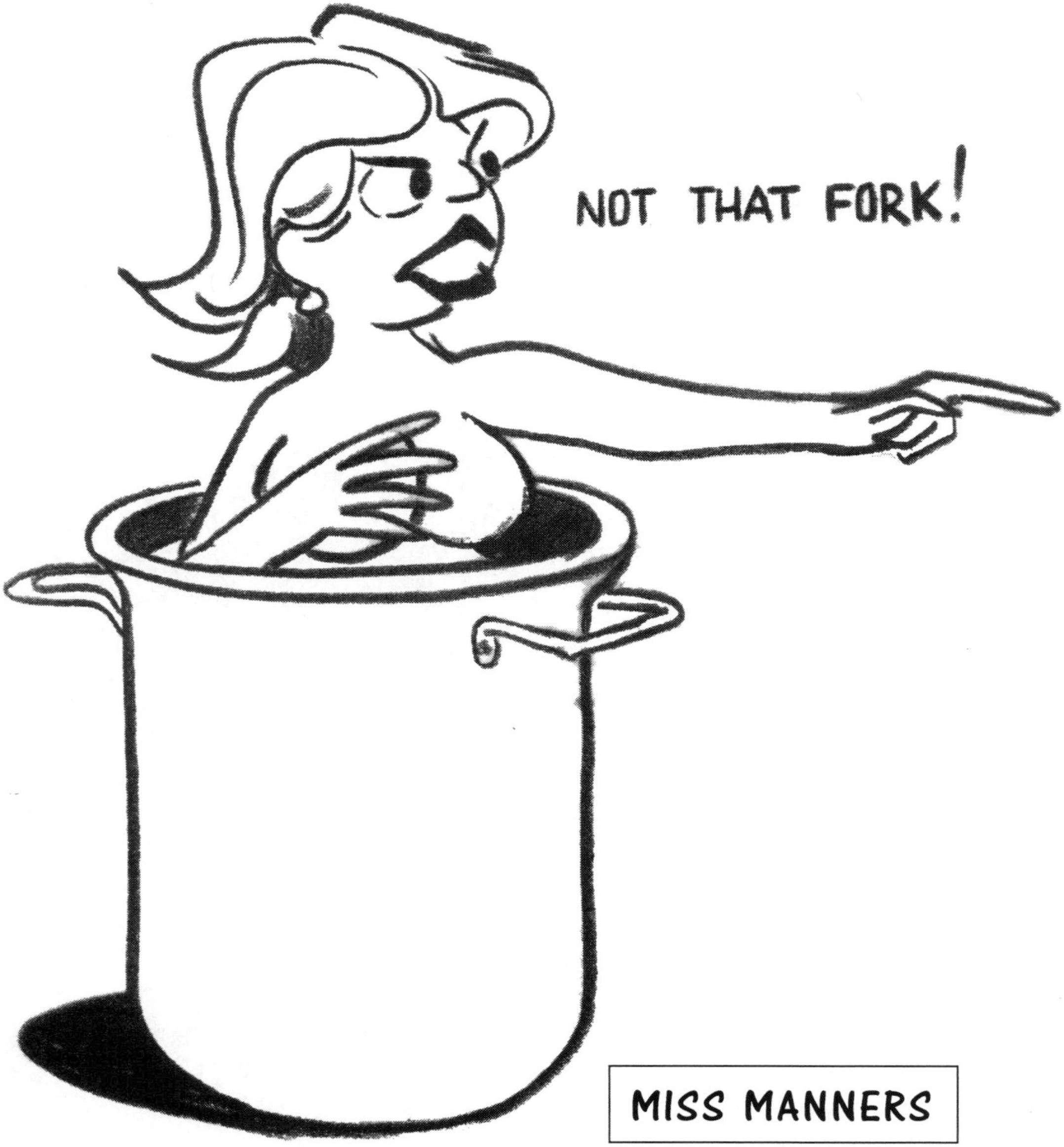
NOT THAT FORK!

MISS MANNERS

Book Reviews

There are many wonderful books available today that will help enrich our lives as we follow our weight control regime. Here's a sampling of but a few:

Miss Manners' Cannibal Code: Providing invaluable information on manners and morals.

- How to address a letter to an unmarried Cannibal lady...is "OTP"* the preferred term, or is "Ms." the better choice?

- Why it's a good idea for executive female Cannibals not to wear power suits.

- When should men honor "dress down" days? Who should they dress down, and how should the dressing be prepared?

- Are phrases like "nuts to you" polite at the table?

- Is the concept "Make love not war" politically correct, really?

- What to say upon discovering that someone invited to a wedding you're attending is a relative of someone you ate? Do you say, "I enjoyed eating the rest of your family"?

- The importance of controlling salivation upon meeting new neighbors — techniques to master.

---
* On the Prowl

The Cannibal's Home Companion

A thorough compendium of practical ideas for daily living, these words of wisdom are wonderful for making life run more smoothly, and they help buoy spirits during those tough moments of dieting as well. Topics from the Table of Contents include:

- Human Society Rules, reprinted in their entirety (e.g., "Rule 23: It is not only humane but prudent to entertain the food prior to cooking at your next backyard Bar-B-Q")

- What to do with the bones — environmentally and politically safe disposal techniques

- Tips on indoor fireplace construction

- Chocolate — its uses in luring prey

- The wisdom of hiding how healthy you are — new perspectives on posture

- Herringbone tweed — a wonderful new way to recycle leftovers

Memoirs of a Picky Eater and *Chewing It My Way*

The first books in a series penned by the famous Cannibal author, Chuck da Speare, these gems score definite bulls eyes. Mixing down-home humor with anecdotes of visits to fine restaurants, both books take the reader on tours filled with gustatory delights, enlivened by fabulous tales of entrées' previous adventures.

A Wine Drinker's Guide

Answers the much asked question, what wines are appropriate for different kinds of people? This invaluable book tackles some of our most ticklish questions:

- What wine does one drink when dining upon an elderly doctor?

- What wine is appropriate when the entrée is a Middle Eastern terrorist? They do not drink alcohol, but does that mean the diner has to abstain as well?

Miss Lonelyhearts

The Weenikit Tribe's own venerable lovelorn columnist has collected the best of her last seven years of columns. Some sample pearls:

- Advice for mixed marriages, Cannibal and Vegetarian — how to cope

- Pleasing your mate after the cookout — a rather racy chapter

- Cannibalism and the single parent — tips on fixing smaller meals, advice on teaching the kids critical survival skills, such as how to tell the difference between a friendly and a hungry glance

- How to be a hunting widow without getting into trouble

- What to do when he continually tells you he's working late

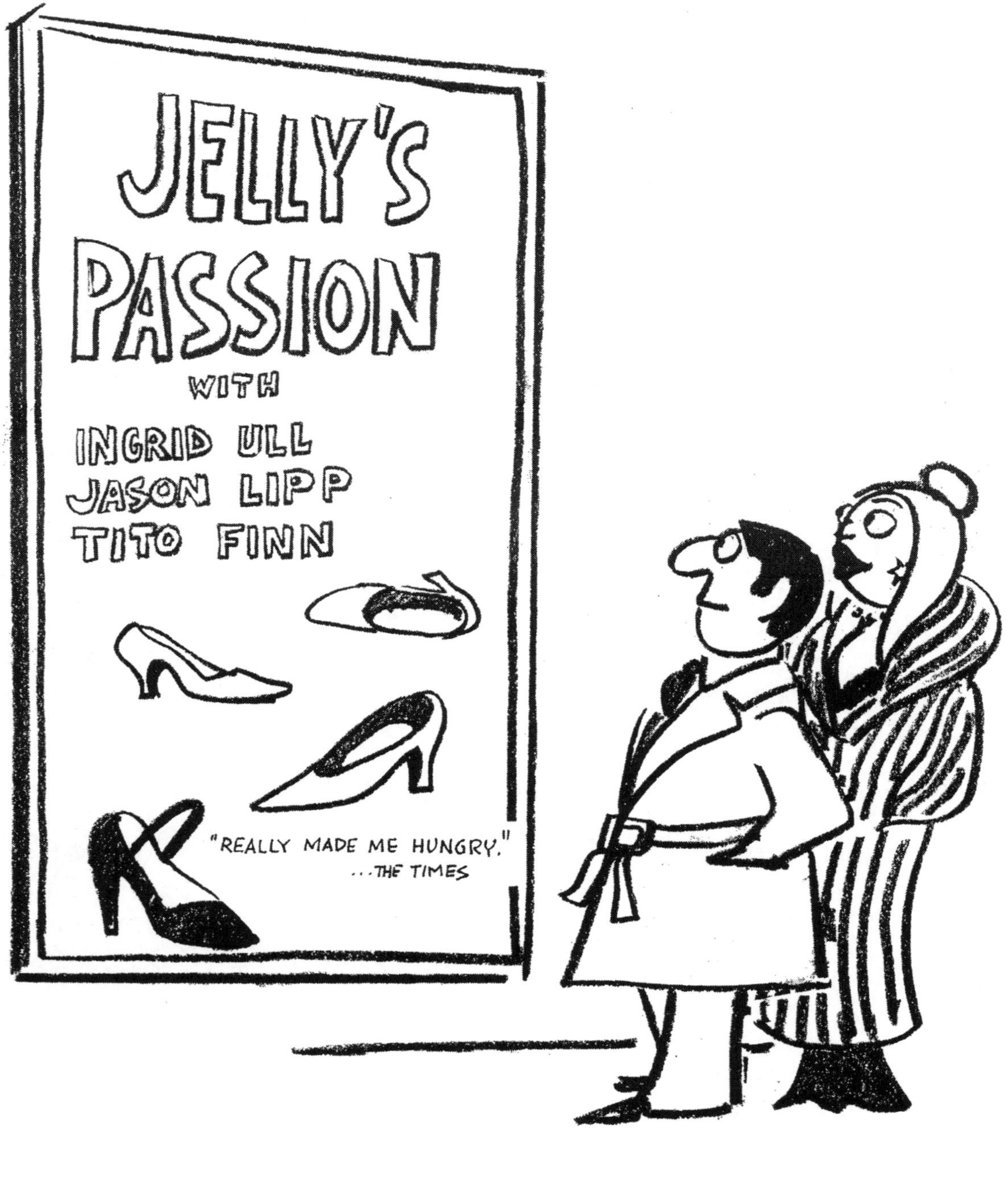
JELLY'S PASSION
WITH
INGRID ULL
JASON LIPP
TITO FINN
"REALLY MADE ME HUNGRY."
...THE TIMES

Theatre

For best dramatic literature entry, the Pulletzer Prize was awarded this year to noted playwright and Cannibal dietitian, Mr. Slymme Gym, for his play **The Girth of a Nation**.

Audience comments following the opening of the new show, **Cannibal about Town**, match this reviewer's feelings exactly, for the first time in history.

> **"Terrific!"**
>
> **"Really made me hungry!"**
>
> **"I especially liked the pickling scene."**

Miss **The Cannibal Follies.** While it is obvious that the music and lyrics were a labor of love, they are Love's Labor Lost. *The Stewpot Bounce* showed some originality, but lackluster performances by Ima and Ura Veggie spoiled the number.

No thumbs on this one!

CROCKPOT AROUND THE CLOCK

Cannibal Top 40: Music for Cooking, Dancing and Exercise

Lots of tunes on the airwaves and rock video these days speak right to the heart —

The Cannibal Anthem — perfect background music for the gourmet cook:

The knee bone's connected to the thigh bone

A big hit from the fifties is back on top!

The Purple People Eater

And from the sixties, that siren song:

I Wanna Fry Your Hand

Fats Waller's jazz classic provides perfect reassurance for your dinner guests:

Your Feet's Too Big!

The Rhythm and Blues classic tells of mistakes we are all subject to:

I left my heart in San Francisco. I didn't wanna do it...

Have you heard the rock classic topping Cannibal charts?

I Can't Get Enough of You

The song, ***Have Another Piece of My Heart,*** recorded first by Irma Franklin, then by Janis Joplin and Big Brother, has been re-recorded by The Youngish Cannibals, and went viral on YouTube this year!

MATING DANCES THAT WORK

Some of our favorite dance tunes

Cannibal crackers in my soup
Plumper than Springtime
Raindrops Keep Falling In My Pot

A real oldie:

"Five foot two
Eyes of blue
Kitchee, kitchee,
Kitchee Koo.
Has anybody seen...

MY SNACK?"

Another oldie but goodie, and a fave:

"Ain't she sweet?"

Post 9/11 hit in Iraq, resurfacing after Obama's Iran Peace Talks:

Un-Cheney My Heart

A Cannibal perennial, from Jerry Lee Lewis

"I hold your hand in mine, dear,
I press it to my lips,
I take a healthy bite,
From your finger tips."

A Maria Muldaur Cannibal fave:

Why Don't You Feel My Leg?

Cannibal Rock Groups

The Ungrateful Dead
The Rolling Bones
The Howling Wolfowitzes

Popular Punk Bands

Sergeants Peppered
The Blue Nuns

From Cold Blood

Down to the Bone

MORE MATING DANCES THAT WORK

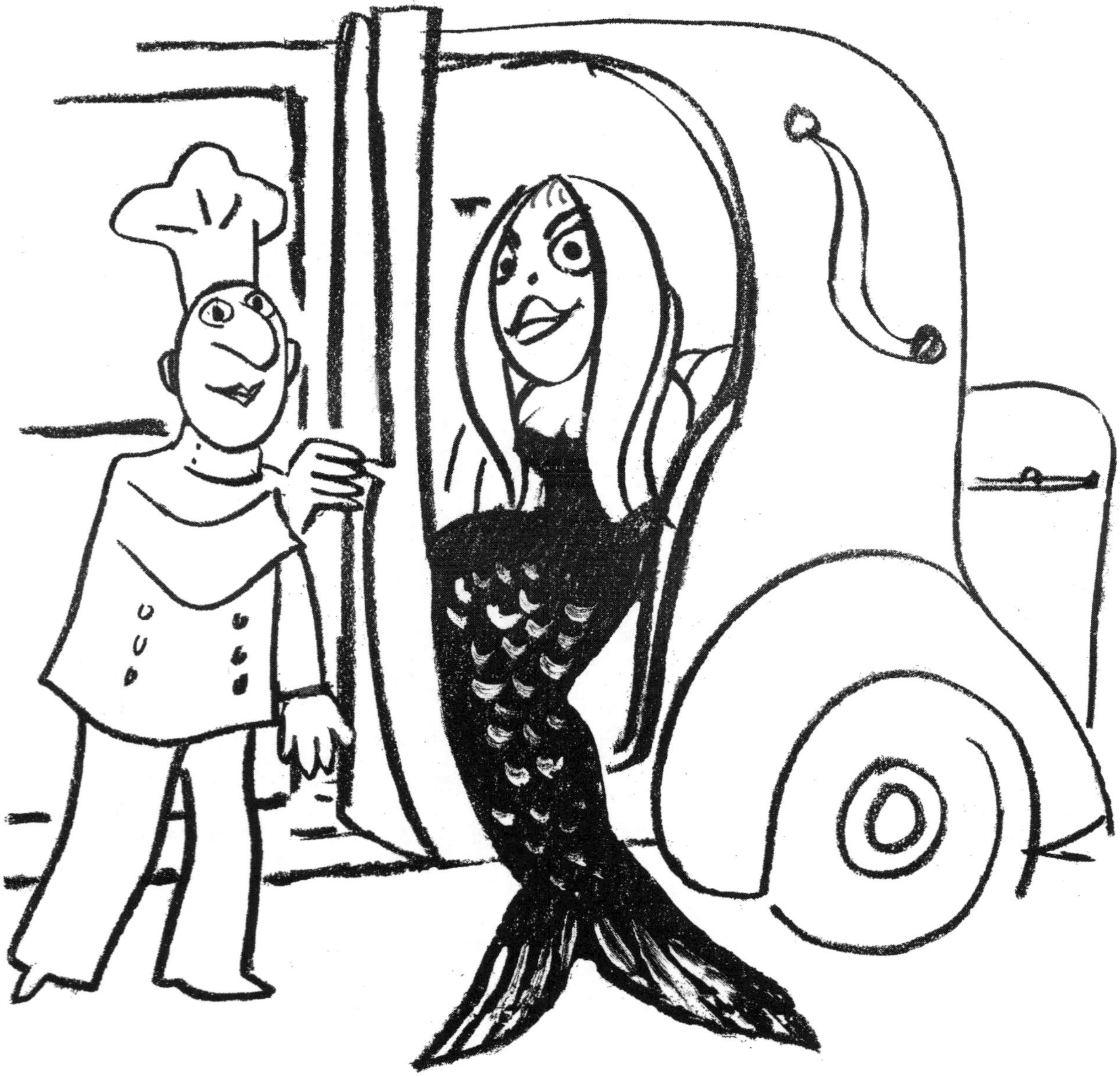

MISTAKEN ENTREES

Movie Guide

Here from our reviewers' desk, a selection of wonderful films to enjoy, and to take your mind off dieting.

The Guest Who Came To Be Dinner

A must-see. Awarded Best Film at the Can Festival. An Uproarious farce about mistaken entrées.

The Accidental Hors d'Oeuvre

A new film by renowned Swedish filmmaker Sven Yborgsen. Beautiful cinematography, superlative acting, with the tragic theme common to all Yborgsen's works. A real gem!

L'Affaire Dangereuse

Henri and Pierre fall in love with the beautiful Madame de Farge. Behind her knitting, they find to their despair, lies a cold, cold heart. The final scene shows Madame licking her lips greedily. Henri and Pierre, for the first time in the film, are missing from the table, their places mysteriously empty.

Transporters

You won't believe the chase scenes in this one! Tommy Le Cruise at his stunt acting best. It's one thrill after another as he goes after prey for a pot luck supper being hosted by BCMF* Gene Hacktheman.

---

*BCMF = Best Cannibal Male Friend

More Movies ....

Cooking Mr. Goodbar

A dark film starring Rip Torn and Angelica Hugestone. Surprise, socko twist makes this a real chick flick. An Oscar contender for sure.

Some Like It Cold

Available on home video. Lots of fun. All about aspics.

Blue Velvet

A cult classic about sex with weird entrées. Explicit scenes.

DOROTHY SAYS
I TASTE TINNY

Deep Throat

A film about two deli lovers who meet in Manhattan over tongue sandwiches. Charming and romantic. We can't understand the X rating this one received.

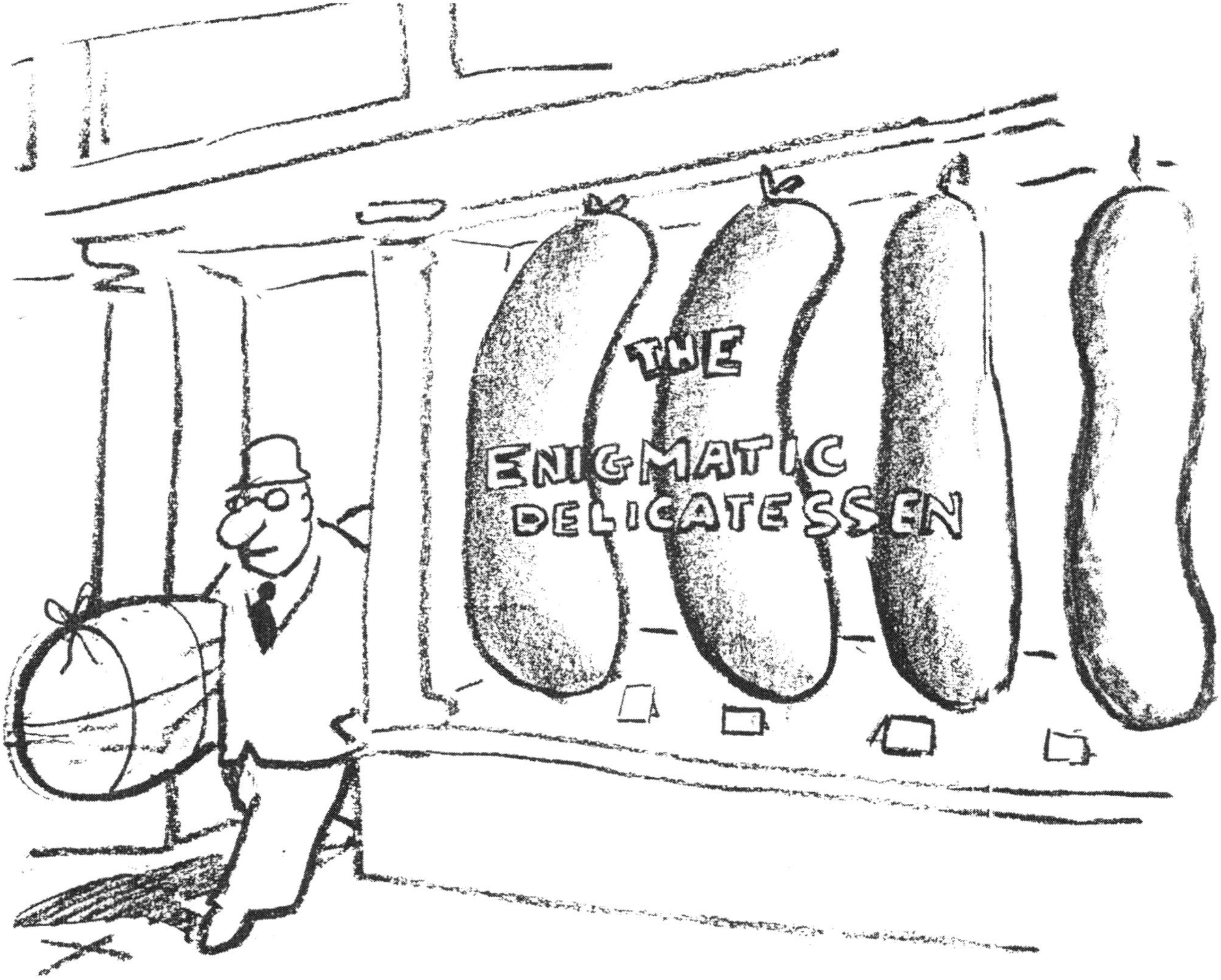
THE
ENIGMATIC
DELICATESSEN

SOMEONE AT THE NEXT TABLE LOOKS GOOD

Dining Out Guide

Piece de Resistance

Go ahead, live a little! Try this exciting new restaurant once a week. You'll want to sample all of these mouth watering desserts:

- Baked Alaskans

- Feel the Bern Crème Brulée

- Shepherds Pie

- Bush's Doing a Great Job Brownies

- Minty Clintons

- Lenin Meringue

- Peaches Melba

- Obamsicles

- Babas au Rumsfeld
  – they're baaaccckkk!

- Trump Trifle

Billy-Bob's Bar B-Q

Billy-Bob's Motto: **We specialize in ribs!**

Great Texas-style victuals in the heart of Manhattan's Theatre District. Created from the choicest anorexics. A real find!

REMEMBER MANUEL'S CHIPPIES?

Food in the News

- The now famous entrée, **Koch au Vin**, had its beginnings in Witchita, Kansas.

- **Creamed Chipped Jeb on Toast Points**: a very light, mild-tasting appetizer, made in a blander, is a recent creation of Chef Gonzales at the new Hacienda los Amigos restaurant in Coral Gables, Florida.

Ethnic Culinary Society Announces Surprise Decision

In a bold stroke, the members of the Ethnic Culinary Society awarded this year's coveted **Golden Stewpot** to Manuel, chef of the infamous Bourbon Street Bordello in New Orleans, for his **Spicy Guacamole and Chippies.**

Excellence in Dining Awards

The **Yummy**, with its cherished bone toothpick statue, awarded annually for the most interesting culinary concoction, went to Mr. Spottem Fetchum, proprietor of the elite International House Restaurant, for his creation:

Peasant Under Glass

FOOD FOR THOUGHT

Famous Sayings

A group of sayings derived from the land of our diet's birth, not unlike those of the "civilized" world, are good standbys when a salty remark seems just the thing.

A Kurd in the hand is worth two in the Bush.

People who live in grass huts should not throw bones.

Mom, who's for supper?

Cannibal mother to her children:

Haven't I told you not to speak with someone in your mouth?

THE JOKE'S ON THEM! I'M A FRYER!

Sweets are neat, but Mandy's handy.

Happiness is:

When a new group of immigrants moves in next to the tribe.

I AVOID YOUNG MEN FOR DINNER -- THEY KEEP ME AWAKE ALL NIGHT.

Abstinence makes the heart taste better.

A spear in time saves nine.

A fool and his stewpot are soon parted.

Beauty is in the eye of the cook.

Two heads are better than one.

Half a loaf is better than a nun.

Make no bones about it.

How would you like a knuckle sandwich?

Her heart is in the right plate.

She had a heart of gold, which was a big disappointment to her captors.

Strike while the pot is hot.

I have a bone to pick with you.

The eyes have it.

You can't judge a meal by its cover.

Cannibal Classics

Authors' note: These are stories we have all heard around the campfire sometime. Reminisce with us now. And trust us – storytelling can be as nourishing as food!

The Witch Doctor

Once upon a time, there was a witch doctor, Har-Poo, a very powerful shaman of the Ug-Tap tribe. People came to him for all manner of ailments, and invariably they were cured. His fame spread far and wide.

One day, a fearsome challenge to Har-Poo's powers appeared. Marty, also a potent witch doctor, from a nearby tribe, burst upon a group of Ug-Taps while they were unarmed, having a barbecue.

Holding a spear aimed at the group, and looking extremely fierce in his war paint and emu-feather headdress, Marty screamed, "Watch it! I'magonnagetcha!"

The Ug-Taps, wide-eyed, turned to Har-Poo as one. He must not fail them now! Har-Poo let out a piercing wail, spun around quickly to the right three times, and spat out the words, "Ug-Tap-it-to-wā-it! Pah!"

In complete shock, Marty fell over. He started to writhe on the ground. Twirling around and around, his body began to change, growing very red and very small. In three minutes, he had turned into an apple.

"Hooray!" shouted the Ug-Taps.

"Not so fast," warned Har-Poo. "There is something you must do now. I have cast a powerful spell upon our enemy witch doctor. But to keep the spell going, we must now take this apple back to our camp and weigh it. And every day, one of you must weigh the apple, to keep the spell in force. Understand?"

And the happy Ug-Taps, from that day forward, performed the ritual weigh-in daily, and kept the spell intact.

The motto of the story: A weigh a day keeps the doctor an apple.

Soup

"Yes, my wife makes a wonderful bowl of soup...We'll miss her."

On Children

"I like children, as long as they're properly cooked."
  W.C. Fields

Definition of a Cannibal

"A gastronome of the old school who preserves the simple tastes and adheres to the natural diet of the pre-pork period."
Ambrose Bierce

NOTICE HOW MY EYES
FOLLOW YOU AROUND
THE ROOM

Balls

Two Cannibals are about to have supper, when one says, "You start at the head, and I'll start at the feet, and we'll meet somewhere in between."

The sounds of satisfied munching having continued for some time, the first Cannibal murmurs, "I'm having a ball!"

The second cries out, "Hey! Wait a minute! Slow down. You're ahead of me."

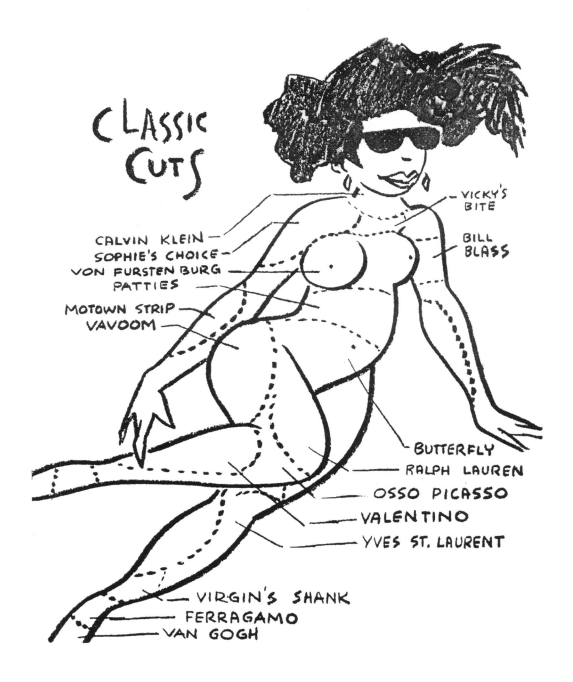

CLASSIC CUTS

VICKY'S BITE

BILL BLASS

CALVIN KLEIN
SOPHIE'S CHOICE
VON FURSTEN BURG
PATTIES

MOTOWN STRIP
VAVOOM

BUTTERFLY
RALPH LAUREN
OSSO PICASSO
VALENTINO
YVES ST. LAURENT

VIRGIN'S SHANK
FERRAGAMO
VAN GOGH

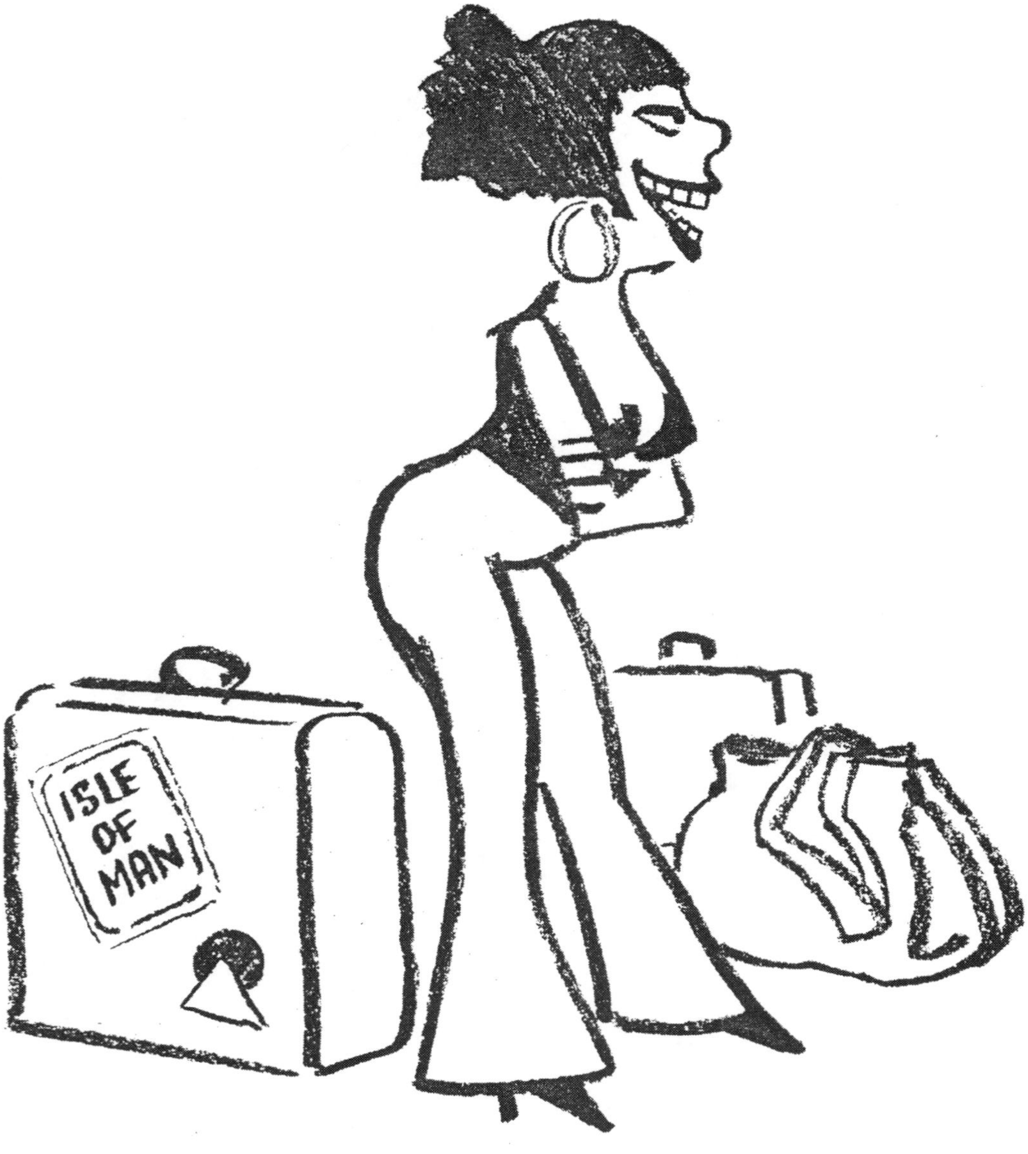
ISLE
OF
MAN

THE FOOD WAS THE BEST!

SOCIAL AND ANTHROPOLOGICAL INSIGHTS

As Cannibals integrate into the "modern" world of nutrition and all facets of daily living, many of us face a terrible struggle. The challenge? How to retain the old customs so important to keeping our sense of self-worth and equilibrium while dieting, without being swallowed up by our adopted culture. Therefore, in an effort to keep alive the history, valuable practices and ethos of the original tribes, we have recorded here some of the most important traditions.

- **One of the most frequent leisure time pursuits of the Cannibals:**

  Jawboning

- **Most Popular musical instrument:**

  The kettle drum

- **The Code of the Great Uneaten**

  In the Cannibal Code of Honor are many old practices. For example, there is the strict policy of the Great Uneaten, which states that if a member of the Cannibal tribe commits a social sin, he shall be left alone to die in disgrace. No one will eat him after he dies in this manner; to do so would bring disgrace to the diner.

- **True Faith**

  Warriors excelling in the skills of weaponry are believed to be divinely inspired, and they often achieve leadership status. A few become ministers of the faith, or *Spearitualists*

- **Travel Practices**

  Then there are the Cannibals who travel all the way to Denmark for coffee and a Danish.

"THEY WERE HEADED FOR CALIFORNIA AND HAWAII WHEN SUDDENLY THEIR TEETH GAVE OUT."

Religious Practices

- In CannibaLand, some tribes circumcise males, and refuse to eat people who eat pork.

- Some tribes take this system further, forbidding the eating of dairy-eaters and meat-eaters at the same meal.

- Hebrews traditionally, at Passover, leave a glass of wine outside for the angel of death, ostensibly to keep the Feared One from entering. Cannibals have a similar practice. We leave a portion of our traditional feast, a rump cut, on a silver platter, just outside our ceremonial feasting place. This ritual is known as "Devil take the hindmost."

- On certain holy days among Weenikits (Wee-nick'-its) it is customary to celebrate by ritual communal celebrations held in a stadium. Posters advertise the event. A typical notice:

  Come one, Come all
  Double Header Today
  At the Old Bowl Park

- Cannibals have resisted outside influences fiercely, especially in religious matters. One rather remote Cannibal tribe, partly agrarian in fact, resisted proselytizing by a neighboring Christian Coptic sect in a rather ingenious fashion. Whenever a Cannibal border patrol spotted any Christians approaching a village, a messenger would warn everyone to disperse with this message: "Cheese it. The Coptics!"

- The Holy Sea Heritage: Meatless Fridays were a blessing for all except the mermaids, but with the lifting of prohibitions on meat, everyone's fair game again among devout Church followers.

- New bans on eating "things that crawl on the bottom of the sea" render professionals such as the Cousteau family and crew much safer now in the waters of the Mediterranean, where this stricture is more routinely enforced.

OH, NO —
ESOPHAGUS
AGAIN

Historical Notes

- Cry heard during the Cannibal revolution in 1462:

  "Let them eat esophagus!"

- A little known fact is that one of the knights of King Arthur's round table was the famous Cannibal, Sir Lunchalot.

- Edgar Alan Poi (Edgar Allen Poe's Polynesian half-brother) introduced Cannibals to oriental style cooking, using pineapple, etc. Poi, a commercial speculator, also supplied Chinese for Cannibal feasts. Many Cannibals were fond of the new Chinese food, but complained of feeling hungry soon after dining.

- Feudal tribes were very firmly (and quite unjustly) ruled by their landed gentry. Even their meals were served in communal pots where everyone had to eat the same food. No choice. No variety. In the year 1315, following a widespread revolt against the repression, many reforms were inaugurated, especially in nutritional matters where food choices were made available to all. This great reform treaty was known as the "A La Carta."

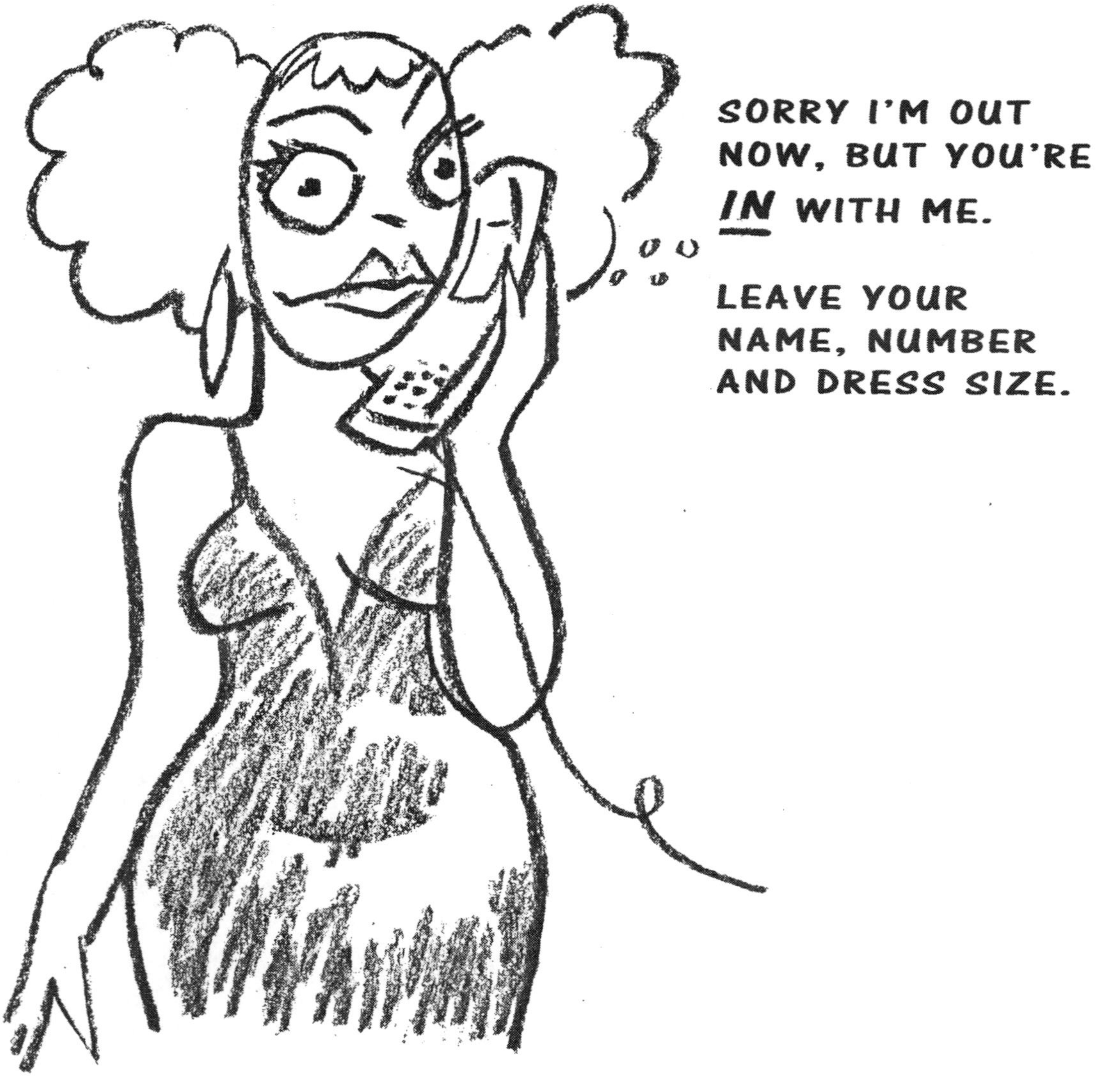
SORRY I'M OUT NOW, BUT YOU'RE *IN* WITH ME.
LEAVE YOUR NAME, NUMBER AND DRESS SIZE.

CANNIBAL VOICE MAIL

Current Social Notes

- How peculiar that most American diners seem reluctant to pick up their tabs, whereas diners in Cannibal restaurants rush to pick up their Czechs.

- Investigating today's trend toward downsizing in companies newly acquired, we were not surprised to learn that many of the new owners are of the Cannibal persuasion.

- Question for social researchers: Is Cannibalism connected with the rise in single parent households?

- Caring for the Elderly

  A new group of Cannibal motorcyclists, just formed in Los Angeles, has come up with a hotly disputed idea they claim benefits Senior Citizens: Meals Under Wheels.

- Children's Treats

  On the Lower East Side of Manhattan, Cannibal kids love the new people popsicles from the Good Human Truck.

- Education

  Changes in our textbooks pushed by Family First And Always (FFAA) conservatives are reframing science and history curricula in many states in the U.S. Teachers are aghast, crying out, "A child's mind is a terrible thing to fry!"

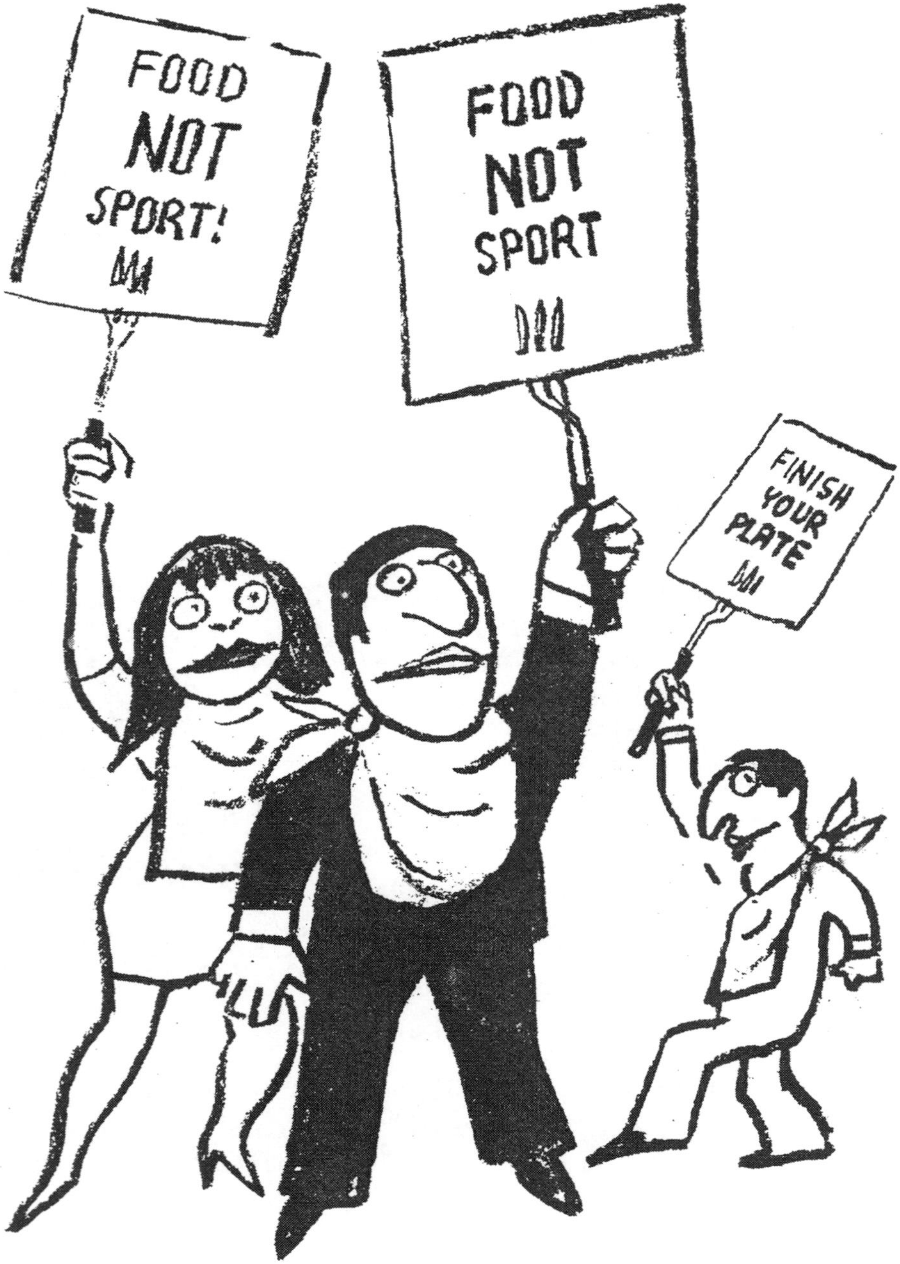
FOOD NOT SPORT!
FOOD NOT SPORT
FINISH YOUR PLATE

Cannibal Values

This editorial is presented by way of explanation about the values — aside from calorie counts — of the new Cannibals, a side few of us knew until now. The piece played an important role in inspiring us to complete this book, for it marks the dawning of a new and incredibly advanced Age of the Cannibal, and a source of pride for us all.

The International Times, January 19, Editorial

A group of Cannibals has recently staged a protest rally against the New Right Arrows Association, (NRAA). Calling themselves the ArrowNoughts, these brave young Cannibals object strenuously to the battle cry of Wayne LaPetrie and the NRAA — "An arrow in every hand," for they have seen it lead to wanton bloodshed.

Maxwell Sheen, spokesperson of the ArrowNoughts, termed the NRAA "Crazy, and wasteful! They kill just for sport, not even thinking of food." Constituents raised their fists in support as he called out his complaint.

ArrowNaught adherents are indeed angrily opposed to the practices of the NRAA, feeling that arming an entire membership is dangerous, their arrow-carrying an invitation to violence. While they admit that in the old country, killing your enemy and displaying his body parts was fun and a sign of manhood, they are firm in their belief that sport killing has no justification in today's world. "Food, yes. Trophies, no!" Sheen thundered.

This paper applauds the ideals of the ArrowNaughts, and supports them in their move toward peace and morality.

Educational Notes

Overheard in a school playground, this dialog between teacher and unruly child:

O.K. You're behaving so badly I'm going to throw you in the pot!

No, you won't, answered the boy. *You forgot you're on a kid-free diet!*

This story just in: from an urban center school suffering huge budget cuts in Texas: Teachers are eating pupils to cut down on class size.

Digestem University Fall Semester Catalog Excerpts

Anthropology 105, *In Pursuit of Humanities:*

A course presented by ever popular Professor Khach as Khach Khan, well known raconteur and bone vivant.

Sample of the many *nutrition courses available*:

Analysis of the four major food chains: Asian, African, American and European

Doctorates are offered in the various cousins*

---

*First cousins excepted; anthropologists have traced this taboo to the first records of civilization, when eating first cousins was considered likely to cause inbreeding, as well as irreversible hiccups.

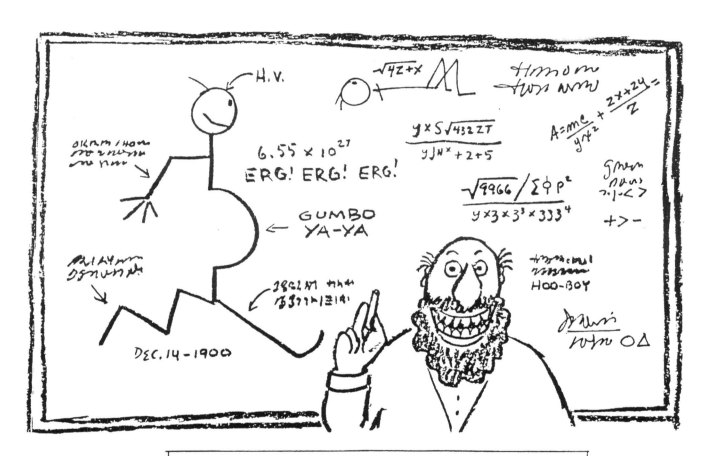

THE QUANTUM THEORY CONCERNING CALORIC COUNT BY MAX (PASS THE PLATE) PLANCK

CELEBRITY MEALS

The Cannibal tenet "You are who you eat" has led to a new trend in dining. Wanting to absorb the excitement of stardom, today's Cannibals are stalking celebrities everywhere. Known usually for taking care of themselves, celebrity meals make healthful as well as thrilling targets.

- Lurking outside the Beverly Hills Hotel, yuppie Cannibals phone celebrities in the Polo Lounge, convincing them that there is an important producer outside, then bagging them in fancy Mercedes limos.

- In Washington, D.C., Cannibals have been seen around The Hill posing as reporters, and promising air time as well as features in print. Many a politico has succumbed.

- Southern Cannibals have been tracking the religious leaders of our country, prostrating themselves at their feet, then throwing away fake crutches, screaming, "I've been saved!" It is an easy step for these phony healees, who offer huge sums of money to the "church," to get the speaker to accompany them in a car, away to their doom.

Once caught, the celebrity becomes the featured dish at gala events. Many now famous specialties have started in this fashion.

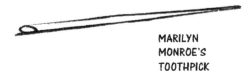

MARILYN
MONROE'S
TOOTHPICK

The notorious Salazar, former Portuguese dictator infamous for his cruelty and corruption, came to Washington to seek sanctuary when there were threats of insurrection. Falling for the scam of the Cannibal press, he was quickly dispatched. Shortly afterward, dignitaries from far and wide were invited to dine on *Soup and Salazar.* The idea caught on, with some modifications, and Soup and Salazars have spread to many countries.

JULIA CHILD
A RECURRING CANNIBAL NIGHTMARE

The following is reprinted from the recent Hollywood gala celebrating the Yummy Awards.

Yummy Awards Celebrity Gala Menu
Hotel Bel Air
Saturday, January 15

Appetizers

Tom Thumb canapes
Rich Little finger sandwiches
Fats Domino pizzelles

Salad

Mixed greens — with Lorne Greene, Shecky Green, Graham Greene
and the cast of *Green Mansions*
Truman Compote fruit salad, with Carnegie Mellon

Intermezzo

Tommy Tune Sorbet

Main Course

Jean Shrimpton, with Jack Lemon sauce
Served with Orson Beans Almondine and the Pickle Family Circus

Dessert

Flan Irma La Douce with Goodbye Mr. Chips
Lollies Parton with Chill Wills
Julia Sugarbaker garnished with Daryl Strawberries

"I MATE — THEN I EAT THEM UP. WHY DO I DO THAT, DOCTOR?"

THE PSYCHIATRIST'S COUCH

Caught between the old and new ways of living and dieting, many Cannibals develop severe psychological disturbances. Some of the disorders are discussed below as a service to our readers. If any symptoms sound familiar, please realize you are far from alone.

Others with your problems have sought and received help. A pre-approved list of psychiatrists is available should you desire. Just write the authors at the address shown in the Appendix of this book. And good luck!

- **Vegehallucinosis:** having visions of vegetables dancing through the head. Especially disturbing for executives trying to concentrate during a meeting.

- **Bulimics** are truly troubled souls, often unwilling to share their plight, embarrassed about it. In our quest to help find solutions, we asked researchers and found that there are certain signals bulimics emit that are really cries for help. Offer to help a friend if you hear her say "I threw up my hand." Chances are good she is not referring to a card game.

- **Alternative healing** is also available. From a recent *Women's Day*:

  "I don't know what came over me. It was horrible. It all started with one finger. Next thing I know, it's all of them...then the toes. I couldn't stop. It was TERRIBLE!"

  If it's always that first bite getting you into trouble, there is help at hand. Support Groups are forming all over these days, and there's sure to be a meeting nearby. Check Google for ***Cannibals Anonymous.***

- **A men's problem:** Symptoms of this disease are most upsetting, and include twitches, tics, uncontrollable thumb-sucking, and rolling oneself up in a blue bankie — all of this happening anywhere, anytime. In seeking a root cause, researchers have published a paper disclosing the discovery that all sufferers ate all or some parts of their mothers. The imminent Dr. Helsig von Freund has termed the disease *The Edible Complex.*

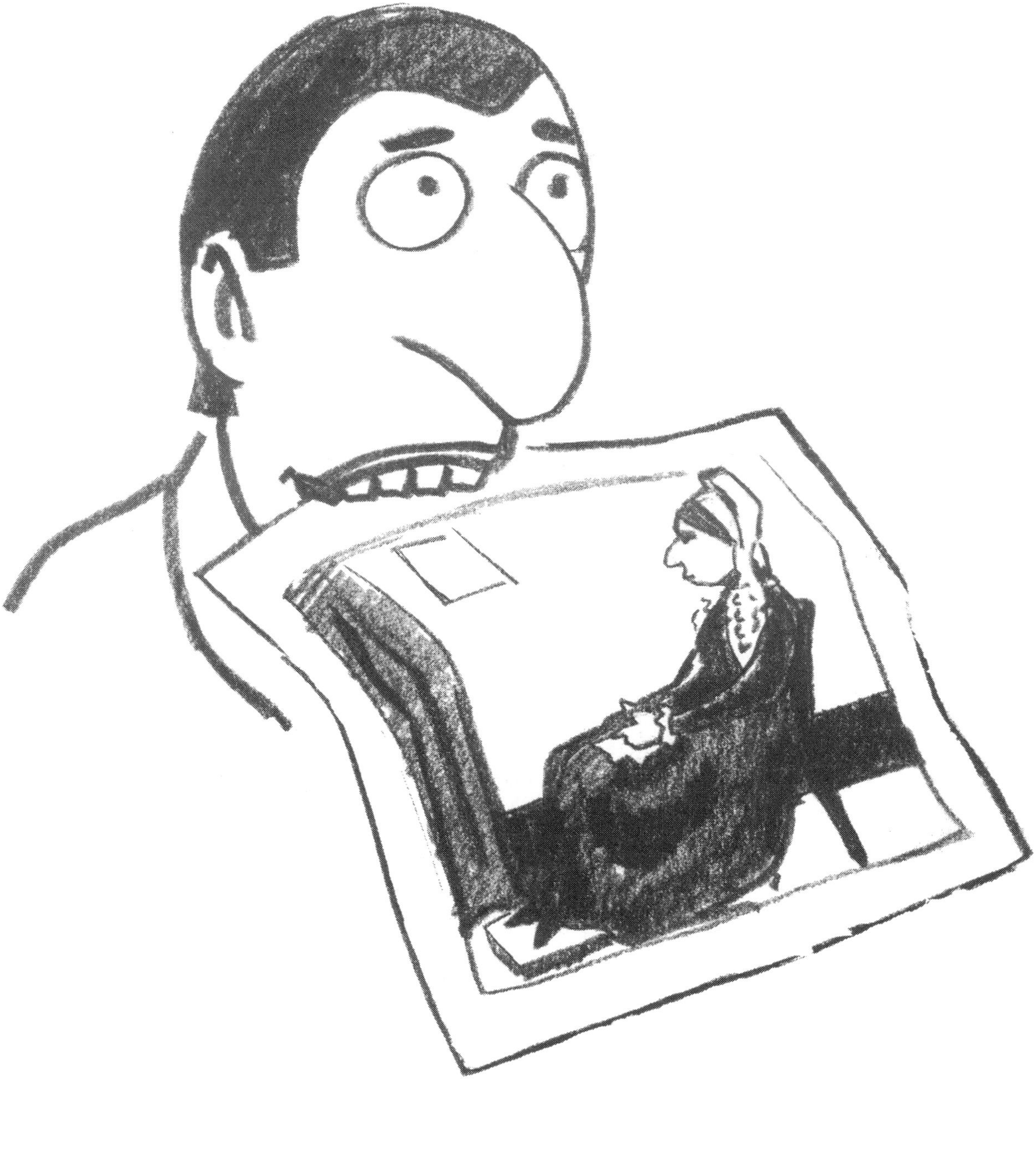

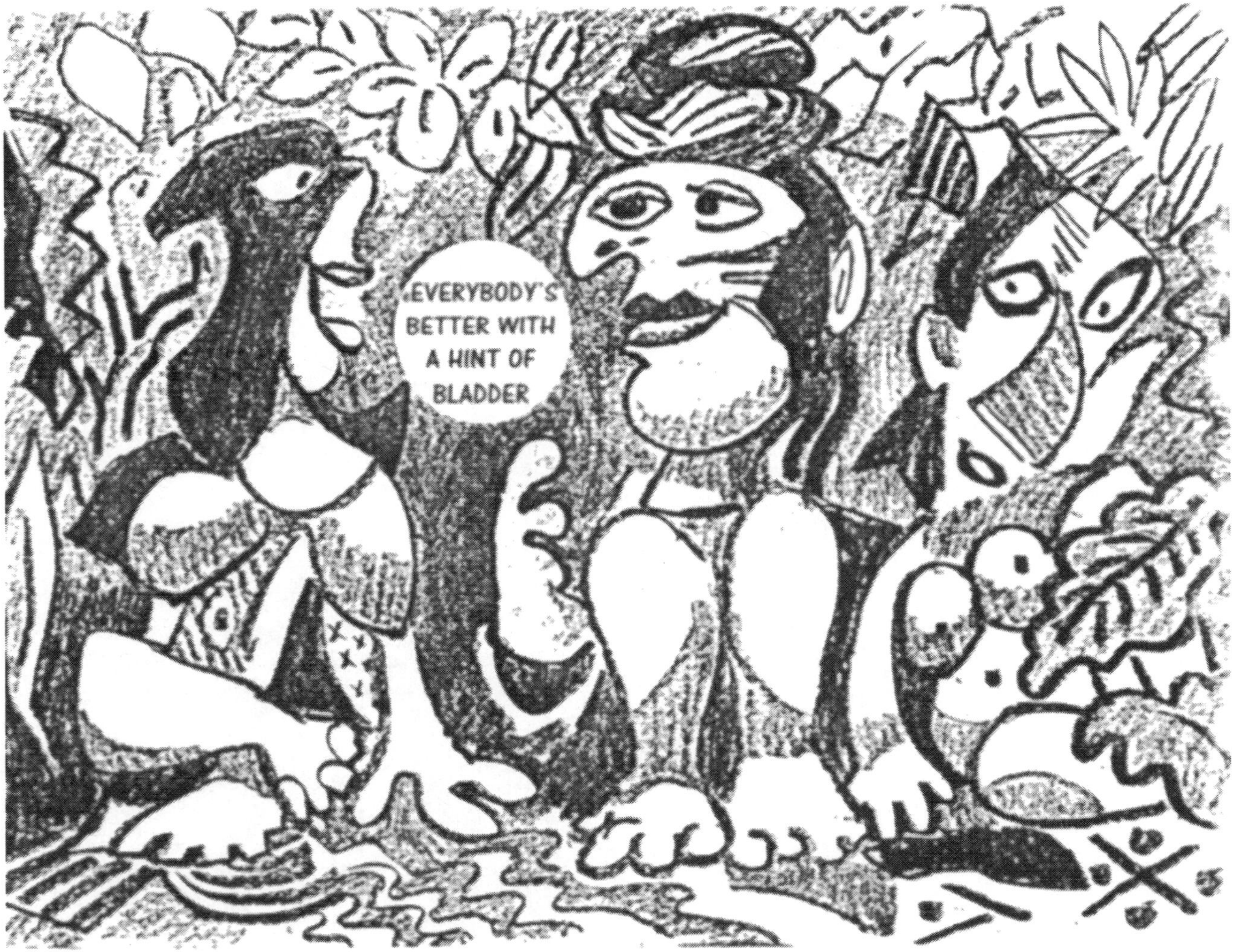
EVERYBODY'S BETTER WITH A HINT OF BLADDER

SHAGGY CANNIBAL JOKES

Elkuit of the Tartuffs (Tar-toofs')

Once upon a time there was a young prince, eldest son of the Chief of the Tartuffs. His name was Elkuit. When he reached puberty, it was his duty to set forth upon a long and arduous journey, all alone, to find his destiny.

When the fateful day arrived, young Elkuit stepped out from the tribe, with a brave face and a heavy spear. His face bore the distinctive markings of the young men of the tribe, white stripes on the cheeks with wisps of blue at the ears. If all went well, the rather silly-looking wisps would be removed and bone earrings would be set in his ears instead.

After five days, Elkuit returned triumphant. Wrapped around his spear was the well-shaped body of one of the Tartuff's oldest enemies, himself a prince. Upon seeing Elkuit, the entire Tartuffs tribe rejoiced. The Chief embraced his son, and both smiled proudly.

"A feast!" the Chief cried. "We must have a feast tonight!"

And the tribe began to prepare for the festivities immediately. In the afternoon, as the sun hit just the proper spot in the sky, Elkuit's blue wisps were rubbed away from his cheeks, and his ears were pierced. Elkuit bore the operation without any sign of pain, and stood tall when the bone earrings were put into his earlobes.

At dinner, young Elkuit, like his father, was presented with the greatest honor of all. That night, and every night thereafter, he had all of his food served to him on a silver bladder.

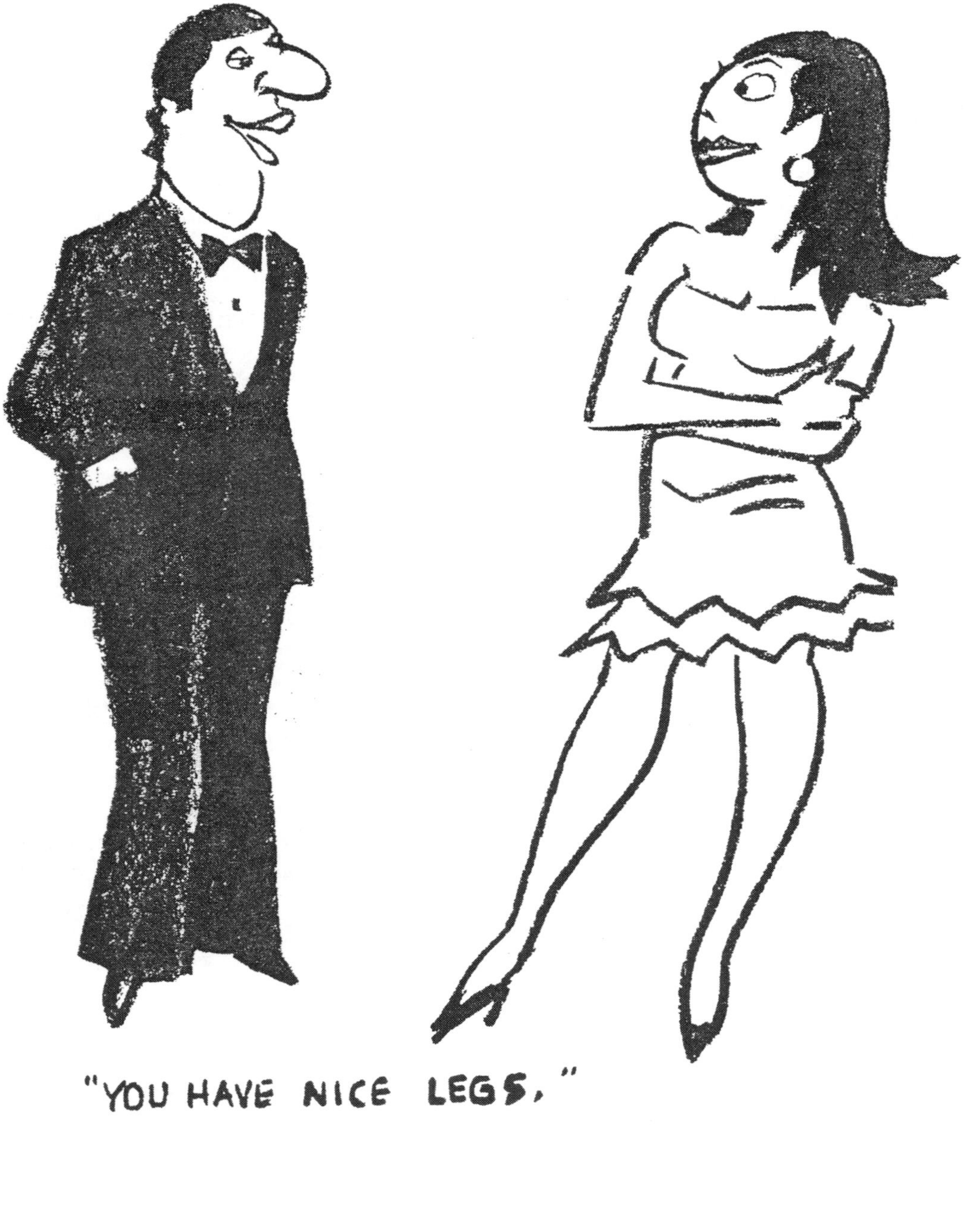

"YOU HAVE NICE LEGS."

THINGS TO WATCH OUT FOR IN CANNIBALAND

When you hear someone say softly, "He/she looks good enough to eat."

Someone whistling, "I've got you under my skin."

Wearing jogging clothes with stripes that glow in the dark when running in CannibaLand at night.

When he starts to sing, "I've only got eyes for you," and you see saliva on his lips.

Be on guard when they play, "Dancing in the Dark."

When someone says, "Thumbs up!"

When the saleslady in the open air market asks, "Are you being served?"

When he says, "Two can't live as cheaply as one."

When the band starts to play, "Two for Tea."

When a Cannibal mother, who happens to be near you, says to her child, "Eat, eat, my child. You're all skin and bones."

When you hear the words, "Eat your heart out."

Taboos

Beware of entering Cannibal country if the name Herbert is on your passport, for Cannibals are always on the lookout for fresh Herbs.

Do not accept if a Cannibal invites you to be the guest of honor at a roast.

Do not accept when your friend asks you to be his best man unless you have a notarized certificate denoting the exact nature of the request.

And that goes double for someone who asks for your hand!

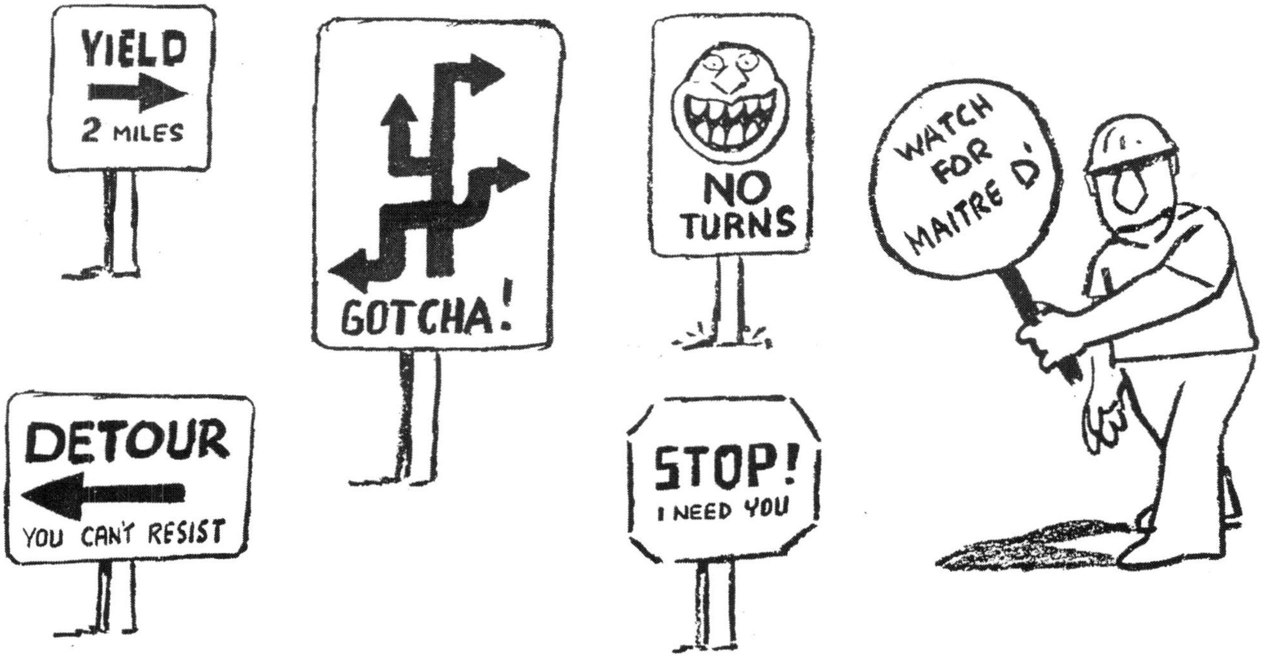
YIELD
2 MILES
GOTCHA!
NO TURNS
WATCH FOR MAITRE D'
DETOUR
YOU CAN'T RESIST
STOP!
I NEED YOU

CANNIBAL ROAD SIGNS

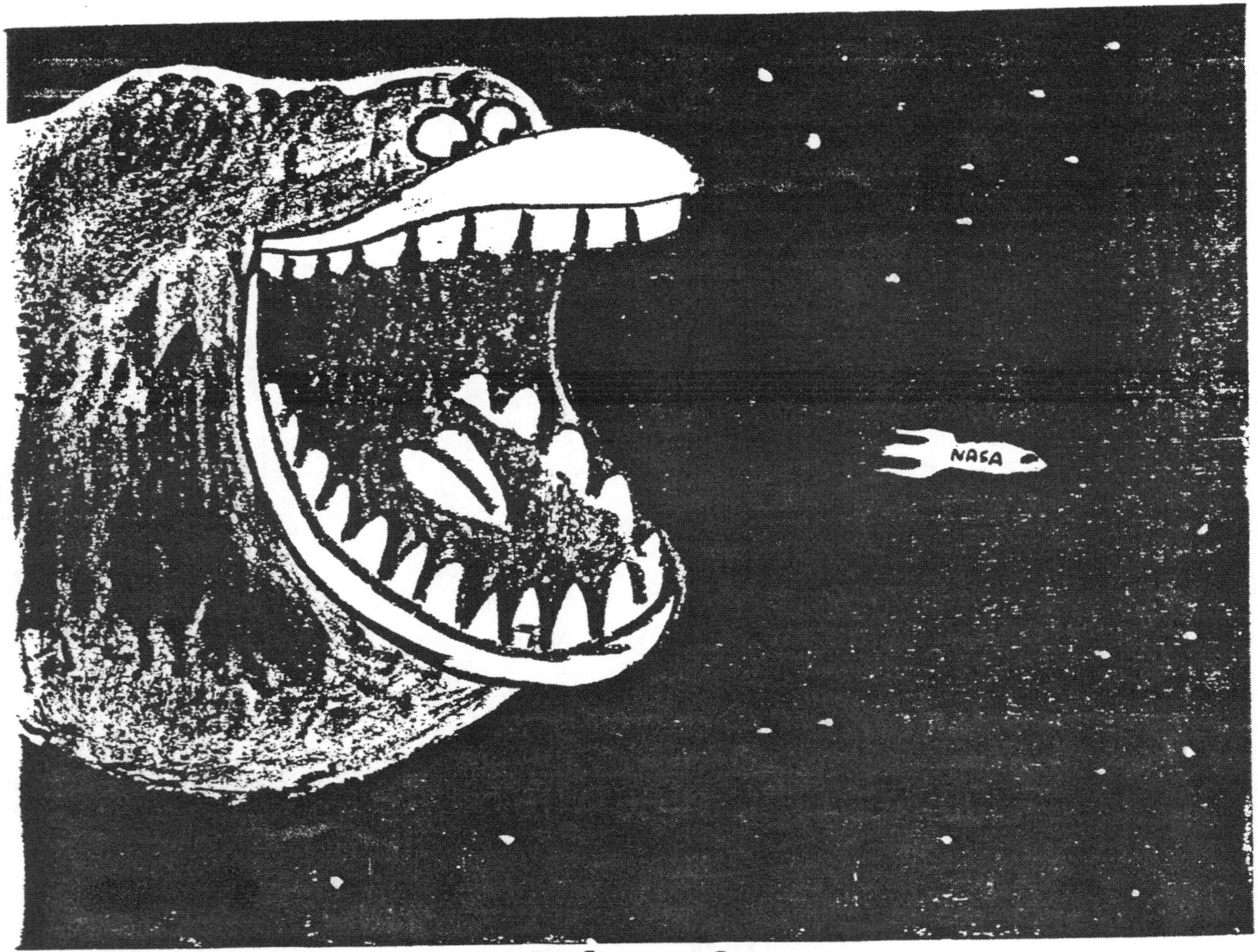
NASA

SPACE CANNIBALISM

CANNIBALS IN THE NEW AGE

The spiritual side of Cannibalism provides great support while dieting. We urge you to explore these New Age pursuits to gain inner balance as you follow your new food plan:

- Aura fluffing — a great preliminary to the hunt

- Astrological signposts — is he the right meal for you, Virgo?

- Harmonic convergence — will you be there for the next great hum-in?

- Throwing bones — a perfect way to detect whether you should broil or fry your catch

- Creative visualization: New Age technique for inspiring recipes suited to the modern Cannibal kitchen

- The sensual Cannibal, power of the root chakra

- Clearing crystals with stewpot vapor, a timesaving alternative to incense smudging

- Know your colors — learn how colors you paint on your face communicate to others who you are, when sometimes it's better to hide the information from your prey

- The Tao of Cannibalism

- Zen and the art of stewpot maintenance

- Ankles and toes --- the hidden mysticism

- Why you should never use the thumb.

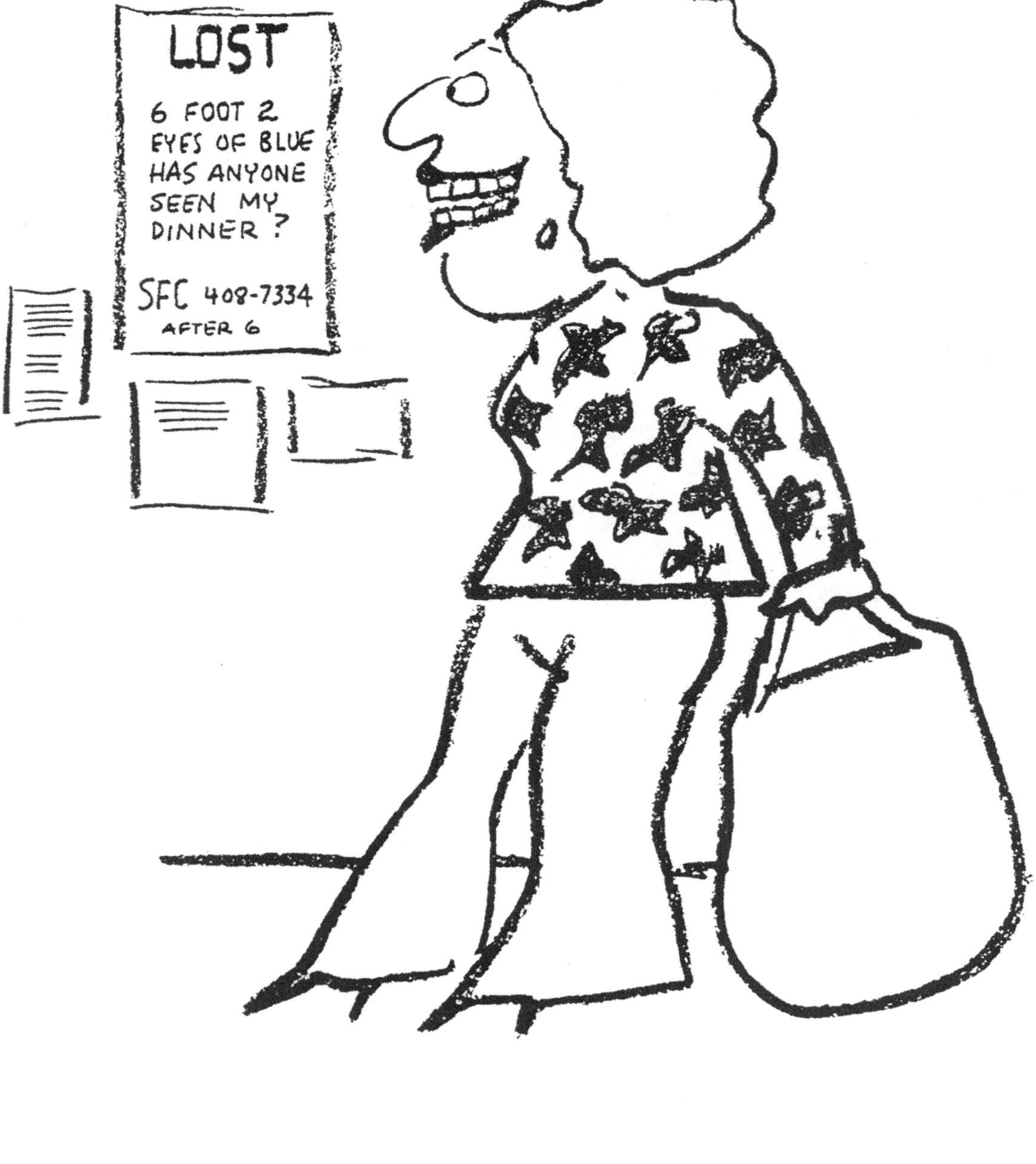
LOST
6 FOOT 2
EYES OF BLUE
HAS ANYONE
SEEN MY
DINNER ?
SFC 408-7334
AFTER 6

LOST AND FOUND DEPARTMENT

As a service for all of our workers and visitors, we feature a bulletin board in the lobby of our offices in Manhattan. For the first time we are sharing these with you, our readers, to broaden our service. Following are some of the most recent board notices. Please feel free to send in any items you would like to have posted.

Lost: One supper, last seen in an Armani suit and Gucci loafers. If found, please return for big reward. First office to your left on 21st Floor.

Found: Recipe for Skewered Presidents. Features clear description of preparation techniques, including proper utensils and tricks for removing stubborn, clinging dirt.

Lost: Prize collection of sacred belly button lint, taken from only the most holy of victims. If you have any information, please call 1-800-457-LINT.

CANNIBAL CONDO

CLASSIFIEDS

Real Estate

Welcome to
Cannibal Condos!
No longer a dream,
But, at last —
A way of life!

Luxuriate in your very own duplex townhouse amidst
sparkling grounds.

Communal cooking by highly seasoned chefs.
All you do is furnish the catch.
It, too, will be highly seasoned.
Or, if you prefer, choose from the mild, not-so-hot pot.

Enjoy tennis, night or day, and golf privileges.

Jump into the hot tub and relax in the sauna,
but be sure not to stay in too long. Some of the
residents have a nasty habit of dropping in
vegetables and snapping the lid on the tub, or
turning the sauna up to broil.

RAVISHING EXECUTIVE —30
LOOKING FOR FEMALE 25-35 —
MUST BE WARM, PLUMP, TENDER,
TASTY, UNSPOILED. LIKES DINING
IN AND NEW JERSEY. SEND
BIO/PIX/PHONE. MBT-N.J. 7052

Personals

SMC* seeks agreeable SFC.** Object, recipe sharing for life. Non-smokers only.

SGC*** on the lookout for the right mate. Your safety assured.

BiCCpl**** seeks SMC, SFC, SGC or another BiCCpl for swinging.

SMC, tender and loving, seeks SFC, under 40, to share love of Beethoven, Bach and Irish stew.

Buxom SFC would like to find strong SMC who appreciates the fullness of life — bawdiness, camping out, Swedish meatballs and pruned Danish.

SFC

---

*SMC = Single Male Cannibal
**SFC = Single Female Cannibal
***SGC = Single Gay Cannibal
****BiCCpl = Bisexual Cannibal Couple

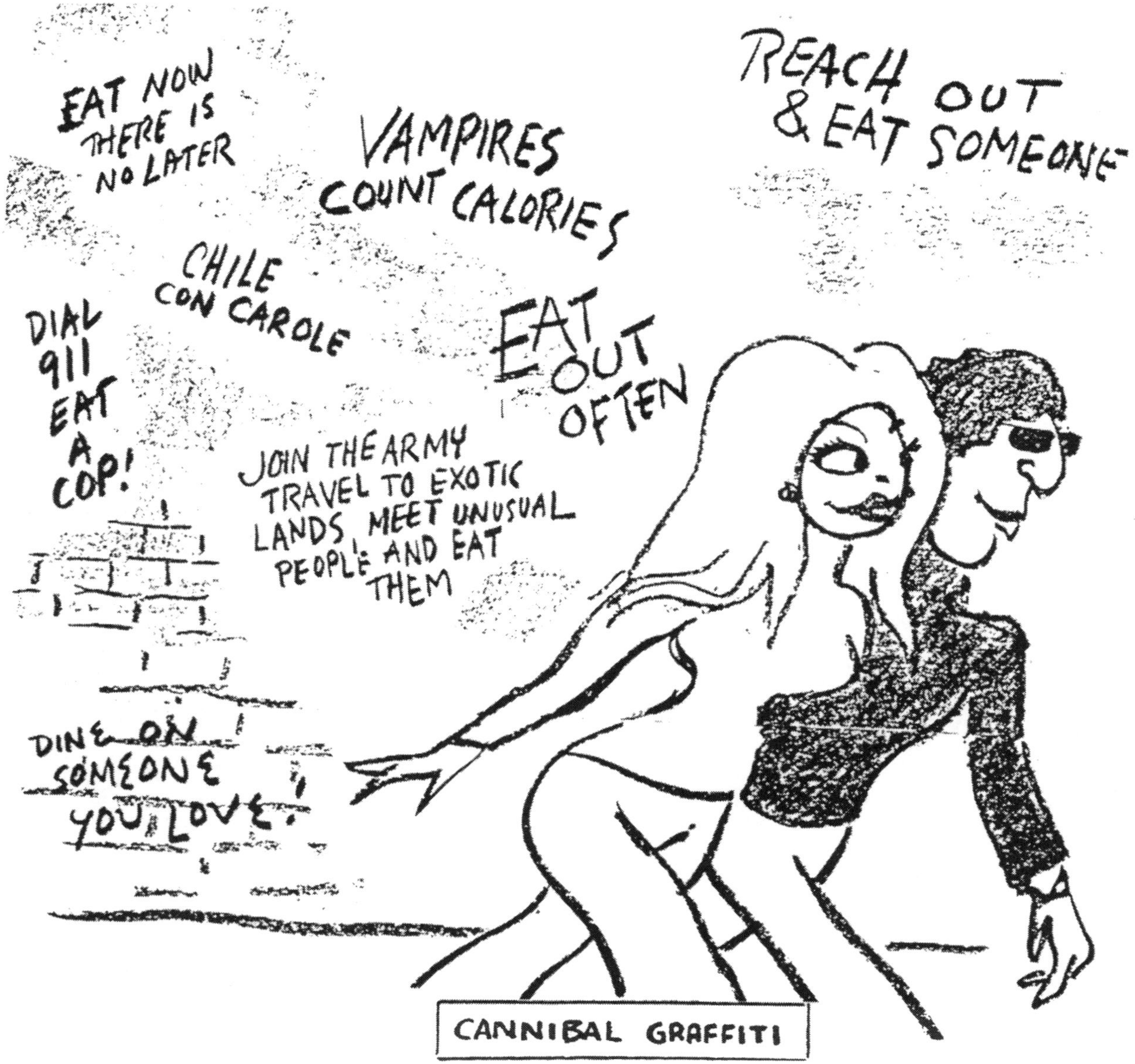
EAT NOW THERE IS NO LATER
VAMPIRES COUNT CALORIES
REACH OUT & EAT SOMEONE
CHILE CON CAROLE
DIAL 911 EAT A COP!
EAT OUT OFTEN
JOIN THE ARMY TRAVEL TO EXOTIC LANDS MEET UNUSUAL PEOPLE AND EAT THEM
DINE ON SOMEONE YOU LOVE!
CANNIBAL GRAFFITI

JUST FOR FUN

What does a Cannibal say when he burps?

Excuse me. It must be someone I ate.

Newly inducted into the Cannibal Hall of Fame:

Buster MacHandric, creator of MacBodies, the fast food chain.

The nickname for Cannibals who eat Frenchmen:

People who eat high off the frog.

Cannibal smorgasbord

Everyone you can eat — $29.95!

WALL ST. CANNIBAL
HOT STOCK TRIBE

The most famous recreational spot in CannibaLand:

Cookout Mountain

Diner to waiter:

Anyone new on the menu today?

Did you hear about the lady who vanishes?

Made the mistake of un-friending the wrong people on Facebook.

Don't forget to try the famous pastry at your local patisserie:

Tammy Faye, Baker's Style

Vicious attack on a comic in a Cannibal club:

Going right for the jocular

A thief caught and eaten by Cannibals gave them their first taste of crime.

An unlucky one:

Always finds himself in a stew.

Sign in a Cannibal kitchen:

Illigitimus non carborendum, or:

Don't let the bastards grind you down.

Definition of a sweet meat:

A tasty delicacy famous as a dessert or snack food. Americans, fed with diets of sugar-frosted cereals, soft drinks and candy are especially popular for dessert.

Most Cannibal health foodies frown upon sweet meat snacks as a dietary staple, however, since they link hyperactivity, acne and other pimply characteristics of Cannibal youngsters to overindulgence in sweet meats.

DINING AL FRESCO

Good Man

The chief: *You know, you can't keep a good man down*

Assistant: You certainly can't. I've been burping ever since this morning.

Hale fellow, well met:

A tasty dinner whom you meet unexpectedly.

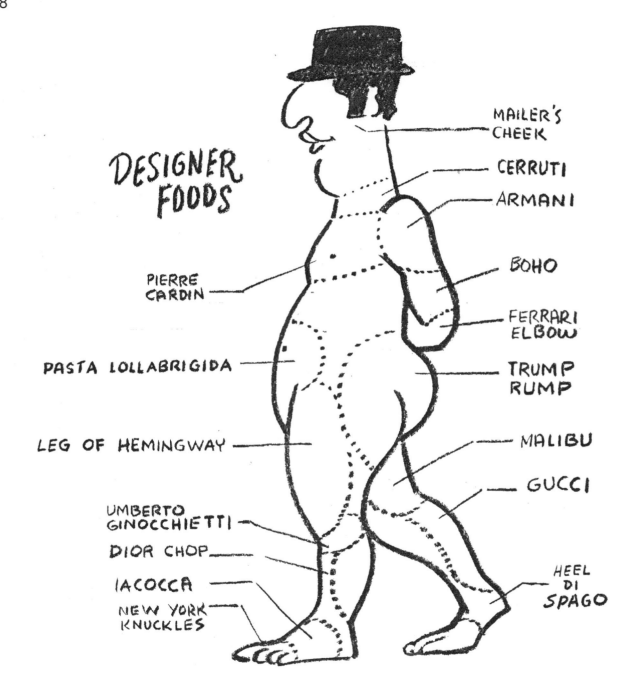

DESIGNER FOODS

MAILER'S CHEEK

CERRUTI

ARMANI

BOHO

FERRARI ELBOW

TRUMP RUMP

PIERRE CARDIN

PASTA LOLLABRIGIDA

LEG OF HEMINGWAY

MALIBU

GUCCI

UMBERTO GINOCCHIETTI

DIOR CHOP

IACOCCA

NEW YORK KNUCKLES

HEEL DI SPAGO

ABOUT THE AUTHORS AND ARTIST
Ina Silvert Hillebrandt, with Uncle Dan — Authors

The authors were born, a generation apart, in a rambling house in Bryn Mawr, Pennsylvania. Early in their lives, they demonstrated a taste for the unusual. Complaining that meats were "too bland, and not salty enough," they nagged their mothers until a change occurred. More and more visiting salesmen dropped in and were never seen again. The young gourmets thrived.

Pursuing their culinary interests, Uncle Dan and Ina both attended the University of Borneo, where they earned degrees in Hunting and Cooking. Uncle Dan went on to become a missionary. Ina entered the Peace Corps, imbued with the altruistic fervor of her Dad, Abe Silvert (founding spirit of this book). After her Peace Corps stint, Ina ventured to Amazon U to continue her studies. The whole family rejoiced when she won the much coveted PhD in Head Hunting.

Later, Ina returned to the States to study with some of the great Cannibal chefs, including Craig Claypot and James Blue Beard. Uncle Dan also returned to the States, moving to Hollywood.to build his new career — spearitual advisor to the stars

It was in a little atelier in Carmel that Ina began her writing career, calling upon Uncle Dan to help flesh out stories for a number of books about their experiences among the Cannibals, most of which have taken place in Manhattan and Los Angeles. She is very grateful to him; throughout the course of their work together he has generously allowed his brain to be picked, though not eaten.

Eldon Dedini — Cover Artist and Illustrator

Dedini was born in a cave in Southern Monterey County. His childhood was spent throwing rocks. For survival and fun. Whatever the rocks hit was boiled and eaten. He called it California Cuisine even then.

The rocks grew bigger, his aim became better, and he slowly worked his way up the Coast to Carmel. Today, his cave past over, he works daily in a tuxedo. However, he still carries a few rocks in his pocket, just in case.

One evening a few years ago, a mis-aimed rock (it's very dark in Carmel) went through the window of a Mercedes and Dedini met the Silverts. Ina stepped out really boiling — and with a bigger rock. A collaboration began. The rest is history.

"I THINK THIS SPOT IS SOMEONE I KNEW."

APPENDIX

We're so sorry. We used to have an appendix, but somebody ate it.

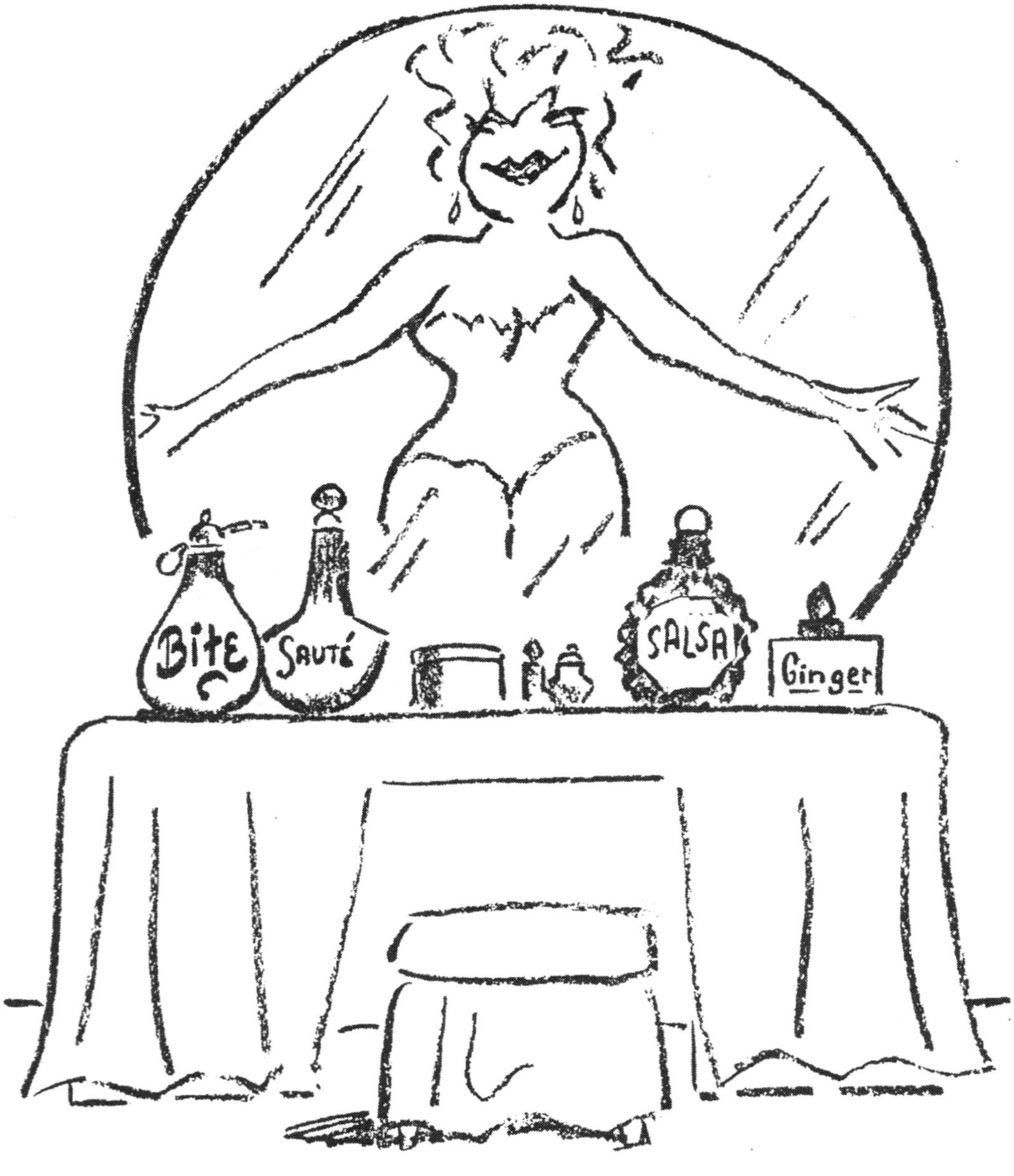
Bite
Sauté
SALSA
Ginger

CANNIBAL PERFUMES

If you enjoyed this book, you might also enjoy the following selections from Pawpress...

Pawprints by Ina Hillebrandt, Amazon.com top seller featured on ABC Nightly News, PBS, etc. From "Moonlit Fox" to "Nose Fur," more than 100 short, short "tails" of close encounters of the furry kind. Uplifts, inspires readers to write, and promotes kindness to animals. Purr-fect gift for animal lovers and pets of all ages. "The stories make you feel you are right there…I love them!" Teresa Proscewitz, Chief Forester, City of LA Dept. of Recreation and Parks. ISBN 1-880882-01-9.

How to Write Your Memoirs — Fun Prompts to Make Writing … and Reading …Your Life Stories a Pleasure! by Ina Hillebrandt. Easy steps and prompts to make organizing those scraps of paper — physical and mental — fun and rewarding, for the writer, family and friends, and possibly, the public! ISBN 1-880882-04-3. "The questions make it easy!" *Gertrude Brucker, Member, Felicia Mahood Senior Center, Los Angeles*

Sensual Spirit…poetry and thoughts from the place where body and soul meet, by Chrystine Julian. "What a rapturous book! Chrystine Julian weds wit and wisdom, body and spirit, in these poems. Her warmth and humor and deep insight radiate off every page." *Gayle Brandeis, author of "Fruitflesh, Seeds of Inspiration for Women that Write," "Self Storage" and the Bellwether Prize winner, "The Book of Dead Birds."*

Meandering Mindfulness…Poetry from the place where wander and wonder merge. Once again Chrystine Julian paints a colorful world of the sensual, spiritual, political and this time, the "silly," in a book that appeals both to seasoned poets and those who usually read prose. ISBN 978-1-0880882-13-9

Stories From The Heart, Volumes 1-3 … Selected stories to delight and inspire readers to create their own memoirs and fiction. Vol. 3 Includes writing tools and carefully selected memoirs — and fiction! — to entertain, and help readers craft their own enchanting life histories. *"Multi-hued, textured tales – from such stuff was woven the American Dream." Marvin J. Wolf, Author of Fallen Angels and many other nonfiction books.* All three **Stories** books compiled and edited by Ina Hillebrandt. Vol. 1 ISBN. 1-880882-07-8. Vol. 2 ISBN 1-880882-08-6 Vol. 3 ISBN 1-80882-04-3.

Go East, Young Man, Go East! *Memoirs of an eyewitness to the oil boom and culture clashes of the Middle East.* By Charles Alan Tichenor, Edited by Ina Hillebrandt. A book of memoirs penned by a witty and informed hand, with tales of political intrigue, spies, cultural exchanges and the effects of black gold on royalty and desert-dwelling Bedouins. ISBN 1-880882-09-4.

Wine, Women, Whispers*,* by Alan Mintz. Tales by a master storyteller who was kidnapped – twice, almost killed by the best hospital in London…A boxer...Serial entrepreneur... Lover of ladies, food and wine. ISBN 978-1-880882-14-6.

Of Politics, Ladies and Bagels, by Gene Zahn, is the product of the fertile imagination and thoughtful and romantic sides of its author. In a wide range of (mostly rhyming) poems provocative to sublime, the reader will find insightful pieces on politics, occasionally couched as potatoes, or bagels; the angst of a young soldier; odes to ladies galore -- often irreverent but never demeaning; and the "bagel's" topping, moving and endearing writings penned in memory of the love of Gene's life, Judy. Available in paperback and eBook versions. Paperback: ISBN 978-1-880882-17-7. Kindle eBook: ISBN: 978-1-880882-18-4.

To order any of the books above, please visit Amazon.com, BN.com, other fine online booksellers, or your local bookstore. For more information, and for bulk orders, please visit our website, http://www.InasPawprints.com. Changing in 2016 to http://Inahill.com

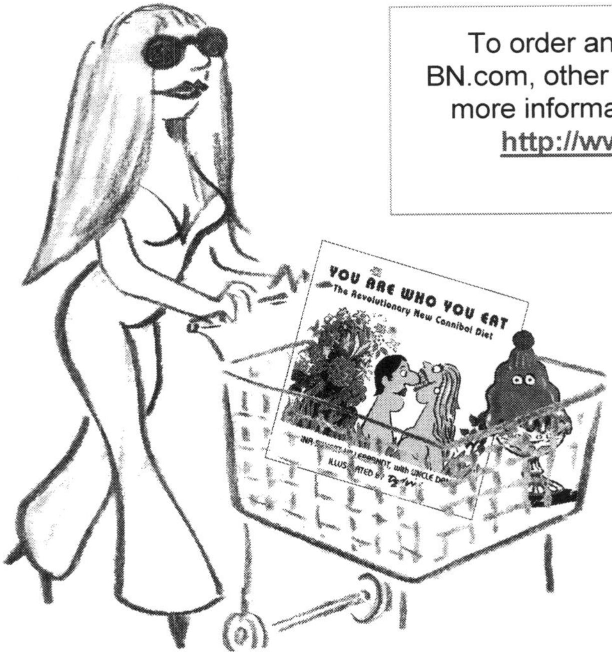
YOU ARE WHO YOU EAT
The Revolutionary New Cannibal Diet

MORE CANNIBAL GRAFFITI

50938660R00062

Made in the USA
Charleston, SC
06 January 2016